NEW YORK REVIEW BOOKS
CLASSICS

ANTI-EDUCATION

FRIEDRICH NIETZSCHE (1844–1900) was born in Röcken bei
Lützen, a farming town outside of Leipzig, to a long line of Lutheran
ministers. After his father's early death from a brain disease, the
family relocated to Naumburg an der Saale. Nietzsche attended the
Schulpforta boarding school, where he became enamored with the
music of Richard Wagner and the writings of the German Romantics,
before going on to study at the Universities of Bonn and Leipzig.
As a university student, Nietzsche gained a reputation as a classical
philologist and discovered Arthur Schopenhauer's *The World as Will
and Representation*, the "cadaverous perfume" of which would hang
over him throughout his career. After a period of compulsory
military service, Nietzsche was appointed to the faculty of the
University of Basel at the age of twenty-four. He published his first
book, *The Birth of Tragedy*, in 1872, but his deteriorating health
soon forced him to retire from academia. In the itinerant period
that followed, Nietzsche completed his most influential works,
including *Thus Spoke Zarathustra* (1883–85), *Beyond Good and Evil*
(1886), and *The Antichrist* (1888). He suffered a mental breakdown in
Turin on January 3, 1889—purportedly at the sight of a horse being
beaten by a coachman. Before collapsing, Nietzsche is said to have
thrown his arms around the horse's neck to shield it from the whip.
Three days later, he wrote in a letter to his mentor Jacob Burckhardt
that he would rather be "a Basel Professor than God." He was
subsequently hospitalized, and lived the rest of his life an invalid
in the care of his mother and sister.

DAMION SEARLS has translated many classic twentieth-century
writers, including Marcel Proust, Rainer Maria Rilke, Elfriede
Jelinek, Christa Wolf, Hans Keilson, and Hermann Hesse. For

NYRB Classics, he edited Henry David Thoreau's *The Journal: 1837–1861* and has translated Nescio, Robert Walser, Patrick Modiano, Alfred Döblin, and André Gide. He is currently writing a book about Hermann Rorschach and the cultural history of the Rorschach test.

PAUL REITTER is a professor of Germanic languages and literatures and the director of the Humanities Institute at Ohio State. His work has appeared in *Harper's Magazine*, *Bookforum*, *The Paris Review*, *The Nation*, and *The Times Literary Supplement* as well as in various scholarly journals. He is the author of three books, and recently collaborated with Jonathan Franzen and Daniel Kehlmann on *The Kraus Project*.

CHAD WELLMON is an associate professor of German studies at the University of Virginia and a faculty fellow at the Institute for Advanced Studies in Culture. He is the author of *Becoming Human: Romantic Anthropology and the Embodiment of Freedom* and *Organizing Enlightenment: Information Overload and the Invention of the Modern Research University* and edits the blog *Infernal Machine*.

ANTI-EDUCATION

On the Future of Our Educational Institutions

FRIEDRICH NIETZSCHE

Translated from the German by
DAMION SEARLS

Edited and with an introduction and notes by
PAUL REITTER *and*
CHAD WELLMON

NEW YORK REVIEW BOOKS

nyrb

New York

THIS IS A NEW YORK REVIEW BOOK
PUBLISHED BY THE NEW YORK REVIEW OF BOOKS
435 Hudson Street, New York, NY 10014
www.nyrb.com

Library of Congress Cataloging-in-Publication Data
Nietzsche, Friedrich Wilhelm, 1844–1900, author.
[Über die Zukunft unserer Bildungsanstalten. English]
 Anti-education / by Friedrich Nietzsche ; introduction and annotation by
Paul Reitter and Chad Wellmon, translated by Damion Searls.
    pages cm. — (New York Review Books classics)
ISBN 978-1-59017-894-2 (alk. paper)
1. Nietzsche, Friedrich Wilhelm, 1844–1900. 2. Education—Philosophy.
3. Educational change—Germany. I. Title.
LB775.N547N5313 2015
370.1—dc23
                                    2015014216

ISBN 978-1-59017-894-2
Available as an electronic book; ISBN 978-1-59017-895-9

Printed in the United States of America on acid-free paper.
10 9 8 7 6 5 4 3 2 1

CONTENTS

INTRODUCTION

IN JANUARY 1869, when he was just twenty-four and a long way from having completed his dissertation, Friedrich Nietzsche was offered a peach of a job—a professorship in classical philology at the University of Basel, where standards for employment were looser than at its German counterparts.[1] Nietzsche was delighted, so much so that upon learning the good news, he broke into song and spent the rest of the day singing melodies from *Tannhäuser*, his favorite opera. The position did have what some scholars might have considered a drawback. On top of teaching eight hours a week at the university, Nietzsche would be required to give an additional six hours of instruction at a local gymnasium. But this wouldn't be a problem, he told his doctoral adviser, Friedrich Ritschl, one of Germany's most renowned classicists. Ritschl passed that message on to the hiring committee, along with his imprimatur, and the appointment was made.

It's likely, then, that when Nietzsche set off for Basel, Ritschl felt confident he had helped launch another brilliant academic career. Yet only a year later, Nietzsche had begun to move away from the kind of philological work that had led his mentor at the University of Leipzig to call Nietzsche the most precocious student he had ever seen: studies on Diogenes Laertius's account of ancient philosophers, contributions to an Aeschylus lexicon, and so on. Furthermore, Nietzsche had started to show signs of deep disillusionment, different from the ambivalence toward academia that he had felt as a student. For all his excitement upon receiving the offer from Basel, he had already been wondering whether the discipline at which he excelled was right for him.

Arthur Schopenhauer was one of Nietzsche's lodestars during his student years, and academic writing, compared to Schopenhauer's, seemed "dead." In the autumn of 1867, Nietzsche outlined an essay —which he would never complete—on Democritus and the "history of literary studies in antiquity and modernity," with the goal of impressing upon "the philologists a number of bitter truths."[2] The first bitter truth was the notion advanced by Schopenhauer that "all enlightening thoughts" stem only from a few "great geniuses," from individuals, as a recent biography of Nietzsche has it, "who most assuredly did not pursue philological and historical studies."[3] Richard Wagner, who in 1868 became for Nietzsche the living model of genius, was certainly no academic. Even while distinguishing himself in Leipzig as a philological prodigy, Nietzsche had considered abandoning the field. But in 1870, he had a new plan, to expose publicly, as he pledged to a friend, the whole Prussian system of education.[4]

The plan came to fruition in *On the Future of Our Educational Institutions*. In a series of five lectures held at Basel's city museum between January and March 1872, Nietzsche took aim at all of Germany's chief institutions of postprimary learning: the *Realschule*, the gymnasium, and the university.[5] He also went after individual specializations, including his own field of philology, which he maintained was both a key symptom and a cause of a larger process of decline. Nietzsche's troubled reckoning with German academic culture gained a new urgency and depth in *On the Future of Our Educational Institutions*. But the lectures have a greater significance than that. Here Nietzsche sets off down the path toward becoming an anti-academic philosopher of modernity and its ills.[6]

From his student days to his last writings, Nietzsche combined a reverence for the classical world, construed in his own idiosyncratic manner, with a skepticism toward modern society. But if there is much continuity to this line of thought in his works, it also evolved over time. What the lectures add—what *begins* with them—is a specific and striking critique of the role of German educational institutions in debasing antiquity and modern culture more broadly. In *On the Future of Our Educational Institutions*, philology and the culture of nineteenth-century German scholarship, or *Wissenschaft*, become one of modernity's most pressing problems. Philology and *Wissenschaft* distort and diminish precisely the resource that might help modernity redeem itself: namely, ancient forms of life. A figure in the lectures remarks, "Philologists perish and are reduced to dust because of the Greeks—that is a loss we can live with—but for Antiquity itself to be shattered because of the philologists!" Here the figure is not merely amplifying the complaint that classical scholars have a special gift to drain the life from their material; he is making an argument that places the destructive tendencies of classical scholarship within a complex causal web, whose strands include an ascendant consumerism, progressive pedagogical ideals and practices, an emerging culture of mass journalism, the modernization of academic labor, the cynicism of modern scholars, and in the middle of it all, the newly expanded Prussian state, which, according to Nietzsche's protagonist, wants to suppress the drive for true education and culture.

Nietzsche leveled his attack on the contemporary pedagogical project within the context of a long-standing debate. Educational policy had been a matter of deep concern in Germany since at least the beginning of the nineteenth century, and by the second half of the century, the German educational system was widely considered to be the best in the world. The British critic, poet, and pedagogue Matthew Arnold believed it was, as did such American educational reformers as Henry Tappan, the first president of the University of Michigan, and Andrew Dickson White, the co-founder of Cornell University.

Arnold, Tappan, and White certainly wouldn't have had much trouble finding Germans who agreed with them. Germany's schools and universities were, understandably, a source of national pride. Its elementary schools educated a greater percentage of the population than their British and French counterparts. The gymnasium, the secondary school that prepared young Germans for university study, was known for its rigorous instruction, especially in classical languages. German universities were celebrated for their culture of academic freedom, for their devotion to the ideal of research, and for the fruits of that devotion: major innovations across the disciplines, from cutting-edge chemistry labs to philological studies and editions still used today. Foreign students flocked to Germany. In 1879, nearly six hundred Americans studied at German universities, a total far greater than the number of students at most large American universities, whose transformation into research institutions was just getting under way. In the United States, rote instruction still dominated undergraduate curricula, and graduate education in the sciences and humanities hardly existed. Thus American students came to Germany not only to master domains of knowledge but also to learn, as the philosopher Johann Gottlieb Fichte had put it, how to learn.

Then again many Germans were critical of the state of education in their country. Throughout the *Kaiserreich*, which came into being in 1871, there was much hand-wringing over the entire educational system. Most of the worries weren't new; they had become more intense and widespread as certain tendencies, like academic specialization, had grown more prominent and as major social changes had taken place. An expanding government apparatus and the resulting labor needs; the acceleration of Germany's economic boom in the years after unification; the pressures that attended arriving on the scene as a world power—these are just a few of the developments that gave urgency to the debate about education, whose central question was: How could Germany's elite secondary schools be reformed to serve an advanced industrial society? Yet many of the participants rejected the very premise of the debate. For them, the problem with Germany's schools and universities was that they had ceased to be elite. In their rush to make education relevant and modern, reformers were casting aside the features of German schools and universities that had made them the object of international envy—their unapologetic exclusivity and elitism.

By most standards, the German system was still exclusive, very much so.[7] In Nietzsche's day, about 3 percent of German schoolchildren, most of them from families with means or with high social standing achieved through education (that is, the *Bildungsbürgertum*), went on to attend a gymnasium. But amid calls to make education more practical, things did in fact change. Educational purists such as the famous historian Heinrich von Treitschke had reason to be alarmed. With the creation of the *Bürgerschulen* in 1859, the Prussian government combined certain elements of vocational and classical education, which is just what men like Treitschke—and Nietzsche—didn't want. The *Bürgerschulen* were *Realschulen* that offered a course of study in Latin and other "high" subjects. They also issued the Abitur, the diploma traditionally associated with the gymnasium and a requirement for university admission. A decade later, just before Nietzsche gave his lectures on education, the *Gymnasien* in Prussia lost their monopoly on being the entryway to Prussian universities. The state wanted a greater percentage of its rapidly growing population to have a postsecondary degree, and now that Germans could attend a university with an Abitur from some of the higher *Realschulen*, total enrollment at German universities increased dramatically, from just over thirteen thousand students in the late 1860s to about thirty thousand by the mid-1880s. The growth was such that the government went from encouraging the expansion of the student body to worrying about whether there was "an overproduction of the educated," as Prussia's minister of culture put it in 1882, and considering ways to quiet the boom.[8]

But not every field benefited equally from the changes. With students coming into the system from vocationally oriented *Realschulen*, and with politicians and business leaders encouraging young people to seek advanced scientific training, Prussia's universities saw the humanities' share of enrollment decline during the 1870s from 60 percent of the total to just over 53.5 percent, while in mathematics and the natural sciences the needle moved the other way, going from 20.6 percent to 32.4 percent.

It wasn't the case, however, that advocates of practical and scientific training and champions of the classical curriculum found no common ground. The debate about education was a complex affair, its dynamics marked by both divisiveness and points where the positions of the various sides converged. Many scientists—for example, the great pathologist Rudolf Virchow—agitated not only for bolstering the math and science curricula at the secondary-school level but also for maintaining the most exacting standards of instruction in the classical languages. Moreover, commentators as thoroughly dissimilar as Nietzsche and Wilhelm II (who as kaiser would say, "I want soldiers not students") shared certain objections to how classical culture was being taught. Speaking to his audience in Basel, Nietzsche had his old philosopher, a character whose voice and views will dominate the lectures, decry such teachers for producing, "at best...little Sanskritists, or etymological Roman candles," whose scholarship he compared "to the hypertrophied swelling of an unhealthy body." Not long thereafter, Wilhelm II lamented the "fanatical scalpel" of gymnasium philologists and its deadening effects.

The specialized character of instruction at German gymnasiums was, in part, a consequence of the Prussian educational reforms of the early nineteenth century, which had required that gymnasium teachers study philology at the university level. This had what Suzanne L. Marchand has described as a "regrettable ripple effect on secondary education." Gymnasium teachers "tended to hand on the specialized text-interpretive skills and detail-fetishism they learned in the seminar to their young students."[9]

One of Nietzsche's original contributions to the education debate was to link concerns about specialization to broader cultural changes, such as the growing power and prestige of journalism. But he was hardly alone in treating the relentless attraction—or, in his view, distraction—of modern journalism as being a force that simultaneously drove and was propelled by the decline of "true learning," by which he meant self-transformation through disciplined, passionate engagement with "the best that has been said and thought." Nietzsche's disaffected gymnasium teacher, younger companion to the old philosopher, doubts that school reforms will do much good, because as soon as students leave class, they "reach for a newspaper."

Students are not alone in doing so. The younger companion argues that specialization compels academics to process vast amounts of knowledge about a small area, making it next to impossible for them to address the bigger picture. Thus it now falls to journalists to give answers to the questions that really matter, and like most everyone else, academics have come to rely on journalists to do that for them. Whether or not the younger companion's point works as an explanation for the importance of cultural journalism in late nineteenth-century Germany, there is something to the portrait he draws of German universities. The system of disciplinary specialization for which German academic culture was known—and which foreign scholars eyed with envy—did in fact lead to a sense of impoverishment and a crisis of purpose among academics, especially in the fields we now group together under the heading of "humanities."

When Wilhelm von Humboldt, a Prussian man of letters, a pedagogical theorist, and an agile bureaucrat, set out to reform Prussia's schools and establish the University of Berlin earlier in the century, he braided together the neo-humanistic ideal of broad intellectual and ethical self-development—*Bildung*—with modern notions of specialized scholarship and research: *Wissenschaft* and *Forschung*. This configuration, however, proved difficult to sustain because, ironically enough, it was so successful in helping to establish the research seminar as the center of university education. Humboldt and contemporaries such as Friedrich Schleiermacher imagined professors and students challenging each other in a relationship of first among equals, with professors benefiting from the nimbleness of young minds and students gaining, above all, the *Bildung* purported to come with focused intellectual exploration. The seminars certainly helped German professors, not only in the humanities but also in mathematics and the natural sciences, to excel. And yet as these professors strove, in accordance with new standards of promotion, to produce the kind of original, specialized research that would make them credentialed experts in their field, the atmosphere of open exchange and the sense of the unity of knowledge, which Humboldt and his peers had so prized, became hard to come by.

Soon the research seminar began to function as *the* chief site of academic specialization and professionalization.[10] Nineteenth-century scholars still argued that the seminars helped build character; in order to thrive, didn't students need to acquire precision and reliability, precisely the virtues that scholarship was uniquely good at fostering? Yet for some, such character formation was an etiolated remnant of Humboldtian *Bildung*. Humboldt himself didn't see the university student's participation in the pursuit of *Wissenschaft* primarily as training for a career in academia. Rather, university study should advance a process of mental cultivation that would make people more effective professionals and would thus benefit the state, but that was ultimately about the flourishing of much more: one's humanity. Though always conceived of by Humboldt as an end in itself, *Wissenschaft* was thought to form young minds. But by the middle of the century, students were being formed, as Nietzsche put it, into "servants" of a *Wissenschaft* that was more a bureaucratic system than a way of life.

As academic disciplines grew to be more specialized and professionalized, they veered toward insularity and fragmentation. And philology led the way. It was the philologist August Böckh who, in 1812, launched the modern research seminar. Within a decade, the field of philology had begun to abandon traditional humanist concerns with the good life and civic virtue, focusing instead on reconstructing ancient passages, methodological questions, and technical debates that only a small circle of experts could follow. "We're turning out men who know everything about laying the foundations," worried one German philologist in 1820, "but forget to build the temple."[11]

"Universal geniuses," or discipline-crossing men of letters such as Humboldt, all but disappeared as mastery of the "scientific" methods of a particular field emerged as the core characteristic of the modern scholar. Gradually German scholars began to theorize about the incommensurability of different branches of knowledge; the idealist philosophical systems that had underwritten much early nineteenth-century thinking about *Wissenschaft* lost their purchase; and the meaning-bearing ideal of the unity of all knowledge was ever more difficult to sustain. And yet many German scholars couldn't fully move on from it either. Longing to treat their work as a part of an organic, if not exactly visible whole, but unable to, they felt shrunken and unmoored. They had been reduced, in the lugubrious words of Theodor Mommsen, one of the most accomplished historians in late nineteenth-century Germany, to "journeymen" serving no master.

Consider the physicist Hermann von Helmholtz. In 1862, he set about distinguishing between the natural and the human sciences, and in doing so he claimed that the human sciences were the better off of the two groups. Against the background of the state enlisting the natural sciences into practical service, he maintained that the human sciences were engaged more directly with the essential task of *Wissenschaft*: separating "pure" from "impure" knowledge.[12] Yet Helmholtz surely found some solace in the sharp increases in state funding for the natural and physical sciences over the second half of the nineteenth century. Indeed, Helmholtz himself received the dizzying sum of 1.5 million marks from the Prussian government to start a physics institute outside Berlin. In this environment, humanist scholars lost their virtual lock on the top posts at German universities, and natural and physical scientists increasingly rose to the upper ranks of university administration. Humanist scholars thus had strong incentives to cast their research as useful and beneficial to the state in the ways that the natural and physical sciences had come to be, and some did just that.[13]

No one did so more successfully than Mommsen. He used his position as the president of the Prussian Academy of the Sciences, which he assumed in 1858, to institutionalize his vision of big philology, or what was famously termed, at a time of rapid industrialization in Prussia, the "large scale production of the sciences" (*Grossbetrieb der Wissenschaften*).[14] After securing a threefold increase in the academy's budget, Mommsen supported a series of monumental projects. He oversaw the internationalization and expansion of the *Corpus Inscriptionum Latinarum*, which sought to do nothing less than compile all Latin inscriptions from across the entire Roman Empire. It eventually collected more than 180,000 inscriptions and ran to thirty volumes. Mommsen also helped the church historian Adolf von Harnack secure 75,000 marks and a fifteen-year timeline for his project *The Greek-Christian Authors of the First Three Centuries*, the modest goal of which was to collect all of the handwritten manuscripts of early Christianity.

Meanwhile, other humanists responded to their predicament by doubling down on their commitment to traditional ideals, such as that of amassing knowledge for the sake of knowledge alone, in ways that could invite the charge of sterility. For example, Böckh, who was himself a critic of philological "detail fetishism," declared in 1855 that "no question is too small for serious scholarly inquiry."

Nietzsche certainly balked at what he saw as the trivialization of scholarship, and having settled in Basel, he may have thought that he had found the perfect location for launching his attacks against the Prussian system.[15] Basel was a city that German scholars liked to belittle as a quaint backwater and whose patrician denizens were, in turn, highly receptive to criticisms of German scholars. Many of them shared Nietzsche's perception of the new German state as "a force dangerous for culture," because Basel had a strong tradition of the kind of classical education that Nietzsche thought was being overrun in his native country. Indeed, some of its leading intellectuals cast their work in opposition to models of scholarship emerging in Prussia. The philologist Johann Jakob Bachofen, whose style of creative reimagining earned him the scorn of Prussia's philological establishment, had even lambasted Mommsen's mode of "big" classical scholarship, which for him was imperialism by other means. Prussia, according to Bachofen, wanted to turn antiquity into a vehicle for its own glorification. No doubt the expansion of the Prussian power to the Swiss border did little to assuage such concerns. Thus the citizens of Basel, who turned out in impressive numbers for his lectures,[16] were likely to disapprove of most of the attitudes Nietzsche targeted for censure, especially the attitude described by one of the figures in the lectures as that of hating "any education that makes a person go his own way, or that suggests goals above and beyond earning money, or that takes a lot of time." Nietzsche's public audience was likely to be sympathetic to one of the main stands he took in his lectures. If we reduce the value of higher education to the material return on our financial investment, we will impoverish our culture and diminish ourselves.[17]

Nietzsche chose an unusual format for the lectures. Avoiding the charts and tables that filled the reform tracts of the day and detailed how many hours of Greek or biology students should have, he gave the lectures a distinctly personal cast. Yet neither were they a conventional memoir of student days. He claimed to be recounting a conversation between an old philosopher and his former disciple, which Nietzsche and his closest friend had overheard as university students, a conversation that changed their understanding of education and, in turn, their lives. The old philosopher strongly resembles Schopenhauer in both bearing and thought. But ideas very much in line with Nietzsche's are also expressed by the former disciple and, albeit to a lesser extent, the young student whom Nietzsche presents himself as having been. Nietzsche's unfinished series—he never produced a concluding lecture—thus stands somewhere between autobiography and invented conversation. The setting of *On the Future of Our Educational Institutions*—the woods—matters, too. Part neoromantic forest tale, part travesty of a Platonic dialogue (due to a misunderstanding, one of the students winds up wrestling the quiet-loving philosopher's rather unruly dog in the dirt), the lectures on education often read like a literary experiment, and this may be why scholars have neglected them. The lectures abound with elaborate descriptions of the sylvan scenery, which sometimes take on the feel of the fantastic.

The old philosopher is clearly the main figure. Yet it is his younger companion who first develops the argument that Nietzsche sets forth in his introduction, written in the spring of 1872 for the planned book version of the lectures, as the "thesis" of *On the Future of Our Educational Institutions*. The companion states that what appear to be opposed endeavors, the widening of education (through institutional expansion) and the narrowing of it (both by subordinating it to the interests of the state and through academic specialization) are in fact combining to ruin true culture and learning. The old philosopher agrees with this assessment, but he further assails the state's role in undermining true *Bildung*. The state, he contends, wants the educational system to produce mediocrities, not the geniuses who might bring about the spiritual revolution that modern Germany, which turns to the newspaper for philosophical discussions and thinks of literary realism as real literature, so desperately needs.

Some of the critiques offered in the lectures are idiosyncratic; some are conventional. And some are both. The lectures often claim that the path to a true, transformative education runs through ancient Greece. This echoes an enduringly popular mantra of German classicism, and along with Nietzsche's admiring references to the key figures (Goethe, Friedrich Schiller, Friedrich August Wolf), it is why some scholars have regarded *On the Future of Our Educational Institutions* as a work in the neo-humanist tradition of Humboldt.

Humboldt's Greece, however, was not Nietzsche's. Whereas Humboldt revered what might be called the liberal tendencies in ancient Greek culture—for example, ideals of freedom and the harmonious balance of different characteristics—Nietzsche saw and embraced a model for the complete obedience to real pedagogical authority and the discipline that, in his view, education required. By contrast, progressive reformers who saw themselves as championing Humboldt's cause trumpeted the line *"Bildung macht frei,"* which had first become popular as a slogan used to advertise inexpensive editions of classic works.

Philologists, Nietzsche maintains, are in a position to foster a living relationship to antiquity. But they did just the opposite. Anticipating the arguments he would make in such seminal works as *Untimely Meditations* (1876) and *The Gay Science* (1882), Nietzsche has the old philosopher skewer modern philologists not only for deflecting attention from the aspects of ancient Greece most conducive for culture—and therefore life—in the here and now but also for spreading a deeply unhealthy skepticism about Greece. The old philosopher claims that some philologists simply have no talent and should have been pushed onto the *Realschule* track. Others are men whose drive for true education has been so thoroughly thwarted by a hostile environment that they have turned to specialized scholarship as a means of "ascetic strangulation." Whichever group they belong to, however, modern scholars and teachers have come to treat ancient Greece as just more grist for the mill of *Wissenschaft*. They have no faith in the redemptive potential of antiquity, and thus the idea of taking on the infinitely "difficult" task of trying to understand its spirit has lost its allure. Studies that pursue that kind of comprehension will, as a result, seem dated and out of place. The majority of philologists, complains the philosopher, "consider such studies sterile, derivative, and obsolete."

To engage meaningfully with the culture of Greece students would need a range of tools that contemporary education does not supply. They would need a proper "sense of form," which is best acquired through careful readings of the German classics in school. They should also be taught to feel "physical disgust" for the bad prose pervading the journalistic and novelistic works they consume so avidly. Nietzsche's other suggestions for improving the education system include limiting the number of gymnasiums to allow for them to be populated only by "real" teachers and by students who, at the very least, have a talent for recognizing and supporting genius when it appears. For Nietzsche, true education is by nature exclusive, and to be worthy of their name, educational institutions must nurture genius, culture's best possibility for achieving "our salvation from the moment." But while Nietzsche doesn't lack for concrete proposals in the lectures, he's also keenly aware of the difficulty of reform, more so than his reform-minded contemporaries.

The great historian Jacob Burckhardt attended the first lecture and noted afterward that in the end it did not point to a workable way of solving the problems it had brought to light. That also goes for the series as a whole. The philosopher and his companion despair of true education, and the former, though treated as a thinker of substance, is hardly a pedagogical model. He repeatedly emphasizes that he wants to spend his time in solitude rather than with students. There are hints that a friend of the philosopher, whose approach is announced in song, might be an exemplary leader of young minds. This friend is someone whom the philosopher takes seriously as an intellect; and he is embraced, rapturously, it seems, by the students in the fraternity that Nietzsche and his friend belong to. While they listen to the philosopher and his companion on the mountainside, their fellow students remain below, by the Rhine, and sing out the arrival of the philosopher's friend. Nietzsche may well have intended to make the philosopher's friend into a Wagner figure whose climactic entrance occurs in a burst of music, but that doesn't happen.

In fact, the lectures break off rather abruptly. Nietzsche evidently tried to create a fuller conclusion for the planned book version. The sort of ending he had in mind eluded him, however, which is one of the reasons why he never published *On the Future of Our Educational Institutions*.[18]

Nietzsche also underscores the difficulty of meaningful reform by having the two students—as well as the philosopher's companion—overlook what the philosopher takes to be one of his essential points. Well into the final lecture, the philosopher excoriates all three of them for not taking to heart his message about the hazards of prematurely encouraging intellectual independence. What chance do you have, Nietzsche seems to be asking, when you get such results even with perceptive listeners who respect you?

Of course, the sense of a system of education existing in a state of crisis, one for which there is no easy fix, is by no means singular to nineteenth-century Germany. It is a sense many people have today, particularly in the United States. Indeed, much of what Nietzsche says about the German crises finds an echo in contemporary debates about the humanities, despite vast historical differences and the foreignness of his authoritarian pedagogical ideals to most present-day discussions. Consider the positions staked out by Mark Edmundson, William Deresiewicz, and Andrew Delbanco, three of the most prominent voices calling for American colleges and universities to honor the humanist mission of equipping young people to lead an examined life while guiding them toward a measure of civic-mindedness.[19] Delbanco, for example, states that with "economic pressures" bearing down on the system, "keeping the idea of college alive for more than a privileged few is a huge challenge." Even in those rarified circles, sustaining it will be, he adds, no mean feat either, given that "many colleges, especially those high in the pecking order, have gotten too close to the world of money."[20]

For Edmundson, Deresiewicz, and Delbanco—all three of whom work or have worked as English professors—corporatized, status-crazed administrations abet and even celebrate the practical and acquisitive spirit that has become so conspicuous at many of the country's best schools. They would likely nod, knowingly and wearily, were they to read the following passage from a 2013 Harvard report on the decline in its humanities majors and enrollments:

> Research has demonstrated that university disciplines must do at least one of three things to draw the support of university administrators. To be successful, the discipline must either (i) be devoted to the study of money; or (ii) be capable of attracting serious research money; or (iii) demonstrably promise that its graduates will make significant amounts of money.[21]

Yet if Edmundson, Deresiewicz, and Delbanco can seem gloomy in their descriptions of the problems besetting higher education in America, in the end they prove to be fairly sanguine. Delbanco is representative of the group in suggesting that commonsensical moves, such as a renewed investment in undergraduate instruction at research universities, will go a long way toward ensuring that college is "what it should be"—namely, "a place where young people fight out among and within themselves contending ideas of the meaningful life, and where they discover that self-interest need not be at odds with their concern for one another."[22] Students at liberal-arts colleges may be flocking to preprofessional programs more than ever before, but on some level don't many of them still long, like numerous other young people, for humanistic exploration? Just look, Delbanco enjoins, at the success of "big questions" humanities courses in prisons and addiction recovery centers.[23]

Nietzsche was also writing as a humanist concerned with how to introduce students to the classic works of literature and philosophy. Like Edmundson, Deresiewicz, and Delbanco, he stressed the importance of excellent, passionate teachers. Like them, he regarded students (or at least some of them) as being fit to reckon with material that mattered. Indeed, he has the old philosopher effuse over the learning potential of German university students. The philosopher lauds "the honest German drive for knowledge" that resides within them—but for the most part remains locked up.

But with "philologists [having] largely come to the conclusion that any direct contact with classical antiquity on their part is pointless and hopeless," the problem of releasing that drive was formidable. It could even seem impossible:

> A feeling for classical Hellenic culture is so rare a result, of artistic gifts together with the most strenuous educational struggle, that the gymnasium's claim to awaken it can only rest on a brutal misunderstanding. And awaken it in people of what age? Young enough to be blindly yanked around by the gaudiest fashions of the day; too young to have the slightest sense that *if* this feeling for the Hellenic ever should awaken, it could only express itself in a constant fight against the supposed culture of the present day. For today's gymnasium student, the Greeks as such are dead.

How could teachers induce students to open themselves up to material from a culture—antiquity, in this case—that was an inversion of their own? Nietzsche saw the "pseudo-culture" of modernity as defined by the incessant pursuit of the new and immediate, and also by crude, materialistic notions of the good life. Antiquity, for him, stood for everything that modern German culture was not. The only hope for redeeming German modernity was for its most gifted children to understand, through a process of "all-consuming" study, and to embrace the life model of ancient cultures. But their doing so required the very shift of values that such an engagement with antiquity was to bring about. In the absence of the values it needed, where could true education, the means for renewing those values, begin? Evoking this predicament, the old philosopher speaks in grim tones: "Helpless barbarian, slave to the present, lying in the chains of the passing moment, and hungering—always, eternally hungering!" How could teachers hope to revive a pedagogical ideal and its values when the culture upon which they depended was, in effect, dead?

When the philosopher's younger companion nearly reaches the point of total despondency, the old philosopher tells him to have faith. But the philosopher's attempts to console only deepen his companion's doubt. Change will happen, the philosopher avows. It must happen, and yet the ultimate means of change remain vague at best—the "renewal of the German spirit"—and how change is to come is quite unclear. The same can be said of the old philosopher's appeal to German classicism. He insists that the proper study of Schiller and Goethe will help gymnasium students to appreciate the culture of ancient Greece. Yet he also admits that students are basically incapable of reading them in such a way, because modern students are immersed in a culture that stands "in the same relation to the German spirit as a journalist to Schiller." They are moved not by classical masterpieces but by the linguistic disasters of contemporary literature. Students cannot simply "jump" from a culture of distraction and hope to reach classical Greece. They need "a ladder"; they need, as the philosopher puts it, a leader to take them to antiquity.

But the leader, too, "must have a leader." And how are leaders to be formed in an age so hostile to genius?

The old philosopher seems unsure. Indeed, he concedes that for the time being, the reasonable course of action is probably just to push back against the pedagogy that prematurely encourages intellectual independence and to teach classical culture from the limited perspective of responsible "scholarly erudition." The present is so far gone that "the narrowest, most limited points of view are in some sense correct, because no one is capable of reaching, or even pointing to, the place from which these views can be seen to be wrong." With "no little emotion in his voice," his companion responds: "No one?" And with that, both he and the philosopher fall silent, and the second lecture comes to an end. Much heated debate follows. But it ultimately reinforces that dolorous conclusion.

Throughout the lectures, the old philosopher and the disaffected gymnasium teacher hold forth about the ends of education and the problems of education in post-unification Prussia; the two students, one of them presented as a younger incarnation of Nietzsche, are silent for the most part, but toward the end they also chime in. Again and again they return to difficult, trenchant questions that Edmundson, Deresiewicz, and Delbanco don't ask.[24] But they are precisely the questions that could enrich our conversations about the future of humanistic education. Edmundson, Deresiewicz, and Delbanco try to win over readers by affirming the unique value of studying the humanities. The case they make isn't a repurposing of the utilitarian logic favored by critics of the humanities: namely, that the humanities teach transferable skills. It is a loftier position. In the hands of dedicated teachers, the humanities guide students through immersion studies in works that, exotic or irrelevant though they may seem, can change their lives as no other material can. Nietzsche shared this belief, but he was not content, as Edmundson, Deresiewicz, and Delbanco sometimes seem to be, to recite the credo. Before a supremely cultured audience in Basel, he took a different tack, challenging his listeners to consider a number of unsettling possibilities that have relevance again today. What if really opening oneself up to the life-changing study of humanities will often require an initial faith, so that those who already have this faith are the ones in whom it is likely to be renewed, and those who don't might well remain outside the cycle? What if students at elite colleges are majoring in economics rather than English not because they feel they have to, and at the price of suppressing their desire for humanities study, but rather because in the climate of today, the values supporting this faith have been losing their purchase? What if there is an ongoing thinning of the ranks of students with a visceral belief in the power of reflective conversation, carried on across time and space, with the record of human experience—that is, in the core enterprise of the humanities?

Whoever wants to think seriously about the future of the humanities in our educational institutions would do well to consider these possibilities, even if the answers might bring us little comfort. In 1872, young Nietzsche claimed, of course, to be confident that a redemptive intervention made possible by the "purification of the German spirit" would improve German education. But in the end, his faith seems less than solid. The philosopher's important friend, who we are prompted to suspect might be the kind of leader Nietzsche was hoping for, never fully arrives. As far as we know, he remains down by the Rhine among the fraternity brothers. Who he is—or if he is the kind of leader the old philosopher wants so desperately to see—we never learn. Nietzsche and his friend, the only members of the fraternity who feel a drive for real education, don't get to meet him. The four interlocutors remain in the dark, waiting.

—PAUL REITTER *and*
CHAD WELLMON

ANTI-EDUCATION

LECTURE I

January 16, 1872

HONORED listeners,

The topic you have decided to reflect on with me today is so serious, so important, and in a certain sense so unnerving, that I, like you, would listen to anyone who promised to teach me something about it, no matter how young he was—even if it seemed truly implausible on the face of it that he could achieve anything adequate or appropriate to the task.[1] After all, he might possibly have *heard* something true about this unnerving question, of the future of our educational institutions, and it might be this that he wanted to relay; he might have had worthy teachers, better suited than he to prophesying the future—prophesying like the Roman haruspices, from the entrails of the present.[2]

Something of the sort is what I have to offer. One day, due to a combination of unusual but basically innocent circumstances, I overheard two remarkable men talking on just this topic, and the main points they made, along with the whole way they approached the question, impressed themselves so firmly upon my memory that when I consider these matters I have no choice but to reflect along similar lines. The difference is that I lack the courage and confidence they showed, within my hearing and to my amazement, both in boldly pronouncing forbidden truths and in even more boldly constructing their hopes. It would, I thought, be worthwhile to set their conversation down in writing, once and for all, so that others might be moved to judge these striking views and pronouncements. For various reasons, I believe that the present lectures are the proper occasion to do so.[3]

For one thing, I am well aware of where it is that I am presenting this conversation for general reflection and contemplation: in a city-republic that promotes the culture and education of its citizens with uncommon generosity and on a scale that can only put larger states to shame.[4] Nor, surely, can I be wrong in assuming that here, where one does so much more for culture and education, one must think about them more as well. The only way I can make myself fully understood is to relate the conversation I overheard to listeners such as are to be found here: those who guess at once what can only be hinted at, who fill in what must be left hidden, who, in short, need only be reminded, not taught.[5]

And so, honored listeners, I now present to you my innocent encounter and the somewhat less innocent dialogue between two men I have not yet named.

Let us put ourselves in the position of a young student—a condition admittedly almost unimaginable in our restless, turbulent times. You must have experienced it personally to find such peace of mind, such wresting of timeless comfort from the passing moment, even possible. I was spending a year in such a state at the university town of Bonn on the Rhine with a friend my age: a year without any plans or goals, free of all future prospects in a way that seems almost dreamlike to me now, bracketed as it is before and after by periods of wakefulness.[6] That we lived among people excited by fundamentally different things and striving after fundamentally different goals was of no concern to me or my friend. Occasionally it was hard to satisfy, or refuse, the sometimes ardent demands of our cohort. But even this game played against opposing forces, when I think about it now, is like the experience we all have of certain inhibitions in dreams: when you think you can fly, for example, but feel something inexplicably holding you back.

My friend and I shared numerous memories from the time of wakefulness we had just passed through: our time at the gymnasium.[7] I must describe one such memory in some detail here, since it led to my innocent encounter. On an earlier trip to the Rhine, in late summer, I had come up with a plan that my friend had independently arrived at as well, in almost the same place and at almost the same time, so that we felt practically forced by this unusual coincidence to carry it out. We decided to form a small club with a few schoolmates, an organization imposing certain set obligations on our literary and artistic aspirations. To put it more simply, every one of us would pledge to submit something every month, whether a poem, an essay, an architectural plan, or a piece of music; every other member could offer candid, friendly criticism.[8] We thought that this mutual oversight would both stimulate our drive for self-cultivation and keep it within proper limits. And our plan was a success, so much so that, ever since, we could only think back on the time and place where the idea came to us with a certain grateful, even solemn feeling of respect.

We soon realized the proper form we should give this feeling: We vowed that, every year we could, we would visit the isolated spot near Rolandseck[9] on the anniversary of that late-summer day when, sitting and thinking next to each other, we had suddenly been inspired in the same way. To be honest, we were not very strict about keeping our promise, but precisely because we had several sins of omission on our conscience we made a firm decision during that student year in Bonn, when at last we were living near the Rhine, to carry out our self-imposed duty and indulge our grateful excitement. We decided that, when the day came, we would visit that place near Rolandseck with all due ceremony.

It was not made easy for us: Our large and pleasure-loving student fraternity tried as hard as it could to keep us from taking flight, pulling with all its strength on every rope that could keep us tied down.[10] The group had planned a big, festive outing to Rolandseck for that very day, at the end of the summer semester, to tighten the bonds among its members and send them home with the best possible memories.

It was one of those perfect days that, at least in our climate, only this moment of late summer can produce: heaven and earth in peaceful harmony, streaming forth in a wonderful mix of sunny warmth, autumnal freshness, and blue infinitude. Dressed in the most colorful, fantastic attire—the kind that only students can wear, amid the somber gloom of every other variety of clothing—we boarded a steamship festooned in our honor and planted our fraternity's banners on its deck.[11] A shot rang out now and then from either shore of the Rhine, a prearranged signal to keep those living by the river and, especially, our host in Rolandseck informed of our approach. I will refrain from describing our boisterous march from the pier through the excited, curious town; so too the jokes and games we indulged in, which not everyone would understand. I will pass over the celebratory meal that gradually grew more and more lively, even wild, and the truly unbelievable musical production that the whole fraternity had to take part in, some performing solo, some in group efforts, and which I, as the fraternity's musical adviser, had rehearsed and now had to conduct. During the chaotic finale, speeding ever faster to its conclusion, I gave my friend a sign, and no sooner had the last chord howled forth than we disappeared, slamming the doors on what you might call a bellowing abyss behind us.

Suddenly, the refreshing, breathless silence of nature. The shadows were already longer; the sun glowed motionless but lower in the sky; a gentle breeze from the glittering green surface of the river blew across our flushed faces. It was only later in the evening that we were to perform our pilgrimage of memory, so we had made up our minds to spend the day's last bright moments pursuing one of our private hobbies, of which we had so many back then.

We were passionate about shooting, something that came in handy later during our military service. The fraternity's valet knew the place where we liked to shoot, far away and high in the hills, and had brought our pistols there ahead of us. It was on the upper edge of the first low wooded ridge of mountains behind Rolandseck, a small, rugged plateau quite near the place where we had conceived of our club and dedicated ourselves to it. Off to one side was a wooded hillside and an inviting place to sit in a little clearing, with a view through the trees and bushes. The beautiful, winding curve of the Seven Mountains, and especially the Drachenfels, traced its line above the horizon, with the trees near our clearing below, while the sparkling Rhine itself, cradling the island of Nonnenwörth in its arms, formed the midpoint of the scene that was like a picture in an oval frame. This was the place, consecrated by our common plans and dreams, to which we intended to retreat that evening—to which we *had to* retreat, if we were to end the day in obedience to our self-imposed law.

Nearby on that rugged plateau stood a lone massive dead oak, silhouetted against the undulating hills and the open plains. The two of us had once carved a neat pentagram into it, and the storms of the years since then had split and swollen the wood, making it a tempting target for our marksmanly arts. It was already late in the afternoon when we reached our shooting range, and a broad, sharply pointed shadow reached out from our branchless tree trunk across the bare heath. It was very quiet. The tall trees below us blocked our view into the valley. All the more startling, then, were the sharp, echoing sounds of our pistol shots ringing out in this solitude!—I had just sent the second bullet flying toward the pentagram when I felt a strong grip on my arm and saw my friend, reloading, being similarly interrupted.

I spun around and saw the enraged face of an old man, feeling at the same time a great dog leaping up at my back. Before we could utter a single word to express our amazement—I or my friend, I mean, who was being accosted likewise by a second, younger man—the old man's voice rang out, fierce and threatening.

"No! No!" he shouted. "No duels here![12] You students have less right to duel than anyone! Put away your pistols! Calm down, make up, shake hands! What, can the salt of the earth, the great minds of the future, the seeds of our hopes—can even they not free themselves from the insane catechism of honor and its law of might makes right? Nothing against your hearts, but this does no honor to your heads. The language and wisdom of Hellas and Latium have been the nursemaids of your youth—invaluable efforts have been made to illuminate your young minds and hearts with the radiance of glorious antiquity's wisdom and nobility—and yet you take as your guide the chivalric code of honor, the code of unreason and brutality?

Look this code straight on, for once; think clearly; see through its pitiful limitations; and let your reason, not your passions, be the touchstone! If you do not then reject it at once, you are not suited for work in our field, which demands a power of judgment that can shatter the shackles of prejudice and a rigorous intellect that can clearly distinguish Truth from Falsehood, even where the difference between them is deeply obscured, not as obvious as it is here. Go find your way in the world along some other honest path, my good fellows. Be soldiers, be craftsmen. A trade in hand finds gold in every land."

A rude speech, for all the truth it contained. We answered so heatedly that we kept interrupting each other: "You're wrong! We're not here to fight a duel, we are only here for shooting practice. Don't you know how duels work? You think we would face off in the middle of nowhere, like two bandits, without seconds or doctors or witnesses? Anyway, when it comes to the question of duels we have our own points of view—every man for himself. We won't let ourselves be ambushed and frightened by harangues like yours."

This reply, not especially polite either, made an ugly impression on the old man. At first, when he realized we were not fighting a duel, he started to look upon us more kindly, but the turn our words took annoyed him. He muttered and grumbled. When we presumed to speak of having views of our own, he grabbed his companion and turned away with a bitter cry: "A person needs more than points of view, he needs thoughts, too!" The old man's companion burst out: "Show some respect! A man like this deserves it, even if he was wrong in this case!"

My friend had meanwhile reloaded and, with a shout of "Look out!," he fired at the pentagram again. This burst of noise right behind the old man's back infuriated him; he turned again, giving my friend a look full of hate, and asked his companion in a softer voice, "What should we do? These young men and their explosions will be the death of me."

The younger man looked at us. "You should know that your amusing little bursts of gunfire are aimed right at the heart of philosophy this time. Look at the honorable man before you. He has every right to ask you not to shoot here. And when such a gentleman makes a request...."

"Then you do what he says!" the old man interrupted, with a stern look.

We didn't know what to make of all this. It was far from clear what our noisy shenanigans had to do with philosophy, nor why we were supposed to give up our shooting range out of some incomprehensible considerations of politeness. We must have hesitated a moment, indecisive and annoyed. The old man's companion noticed this and explained the situation.

"We have no choice but to wait here for a couple of hours; we have arranged to meet an important friend of this important man tonight, and chose a peaceful place with a few benches here in the forest for our meeting. It is not very nice being constantly startled by your gunshots, and you will no doubt willingly stop your shooting when I tell you that this man, who has sought out a peaceful, remote place of solitude for a reunion with his friend, is one of our most eminent philosophers."

This rejoinder was even more troubling; now we were in danger of losing more than our shooting range. At once, we asked, "Where is this peaceful spot of yours? Not over there, to the left?"

"Yes, precisely."

"But that clearing is ours tonight!" my friend burst out. "We have to have it," we both cried.

At that moment, our long-planned celebration was more important to us than all the philosophers in the world, and we insisted so strongly on our seemingly unreasonable demand, expressing ourselves with such intensity, that we may have seemed a bit ridiculous. Either way, our philosophical gadflies gave us a quizzical smile, as if to say that now we had to explain and excuse ourselves. But we said nothing. The last thing we wanted to do was to betray our secret.

So the two pairs stood silently facing each other. An evening red, poured out across the sky, lay above the treetops. The philosopher gazed toward the sun, his companion at him, and my friend and I at our secluded spot in the forest. That it might be taken from us, on today of all days! We felt bitter and angry. What good is all the philosophy in the world, we thought, if it prevents us from enjoying some time alone with a friend, and keeps us from becoming philosophers ourselves? For we felt that our commemoration was genuinely philosophical in nature: We wanted to make serious resolutions and life plans; we hoped to find, in solitary contemplation, something that would shape our innermost souls and satisfy those souls in the future, just as the labors of our youth had done in the past. That was what we had vowed to do: sit there alone in contemplation, as we were doing five years earlier when we each arrived at the same resolve. It was supposed to be a silent ceremony—all memory, all future, the present a mere hyphen between them. And now hostile fate had forced its way into our charmed circle ... and we did not know how to drive it off. In truth, though, there was something mysterious, even exciting, about this strange encounter.

While we stood there in two groups, silent and hostile, and the evening clouds grew ever redder overhead, the evening itself ever calmer and milder; while we listened, as it were, to the regular breathing of Nature as it concluded with satisfaction its day's work, the masterpiece of a perfect, consummated day—just then a boisterous cheer of many voices echoed up from the Rhine and tore through the twilight stillness. It could only be our fellow students, probably wanting to take boats out to row on the river. We thought about how the others must have been missing us, and we missed them, too; my friend and I raised our pistols at almost the same moment, and the echo brought our shots back to us along with a friendly shout of recognition from below. For we were well known in our fraternity, even notorious, for our love of pistol shooting.

At the same moment, we realized how terribly rude we were being to the silent philosophical newcomers. They had stood there calmly observing the scene until our double pistol shot made them jump. We stepped quickly up to them and alternately cried, "Forgive us! That was our final volley, a signal to our friends on the Rhine. They understood. Can you hear them?—If you absolutely need to wait in that spot in the woods, surely we can at least sit there too? There are several benches; we won't bother you. We'll sit quietly, we won't say a word. But it's past seven o'clock now and we *have to* go there."

I paused, then added: "That sounds more mysterious than it is. We have made a solemn vow to spend the next hour there. There's a reason: A happy memory makes the place sacred to us, and we hope it will also lay the groundwork for a happy future. For that reason, too, we wouldn't want to leave you with any bad memories—even though we have already disturbed and startled you more than once."

The philosopher said nothing, but his younger companion spoke: "I'm afraid our commitments demand that we be at the same place and the same time. There is nothing to be done, except ask ourselves whether this is the hand of fate or the work of some mischievous goblin."

"Well, my friend," the philosopher said, apparently placated, "I am better pleased with our pistol-shooting young men than I was before. Did you notice how calm they were while we looked at the sky? They weren't talking, they weren't smoking, they were standing quietly—I could almost believe they were reflecting."

Suddenly he turned to us. "*Were* you reflecting on something? Tell me, while we walk together to where we will share a moment's rest." We strolled over and clambered down into the warm, shady forest. It had already begun to grow darker there. On the way, my friend spoke candidly and told the philosopher what he had been afraid of: that today, for the first time, a philosopher might keep him from philosophizing.

The old man laughed. "What? You were afraid a philosopher would prevent you from philosophizing? That sort of thing can indeed happen—hasn't it ever happened to you? Not even at your university? You do go to philosophy lectures, don't you?"

It was an uncomfortable question for us, since we hadn't attended even one. And, like many others, we had the innocent belief that anyone at a university with the office and title of philosopher was in fact a philosopher. We were inexperienced and misinformed back then. We admitted we had never been to any philosophy lectures, but said that we certainly planned to make up for it at some point.

"But then what is it that you call," he asked, "philosophizing?"

"We can't give you an exact definition," I said. "But it's something like: making a serious effort to reflect on the best way to become truly educated."[13]

"That is a large task, and also very little," the philosopher growled. "Reflect long and hard on it! Here are our benches. Let us sit far apart—the last thing I want to do is disturb your reflections about how best to become truly educated. I wish you the best of luck, and...views, as in the question of duels: real brand-new well-educated personal views. This philosopher does not want to stop you from philosophizing. Just don't startle him with your gunshots. Today, for once, do as the young Pythagoreans did: they had to keep silent for five years in the service of genuine philosophy—you are not being asked for even five half-hours, in the service of this education of yours that you want so urgently to consider."[14]

We had reached our destination, and our ceremony of remembrance began. Just as five years before, the Rhine swam in a gentle haze; again, as then, the sky shined, the woods gave off their woodsy smell. The most distant corner of the farthest bench received us; there we sat, almost hidden, so that neither the philosopher nor his companion could see our faces. We were alone. The philosopher's voice was muffled; the rustling of the leaves and the hum of the tree-tops teeming with thousandfold life all but turned his voice into a kind of natural music. It reached us as a murmur, a distant, monotonous sound. We were truly undisturbed.

Some time passed. The evening red grew ever paler, and the memory of our youthful educational undertaking rose up before us ever more clearly. We felt that we owed this curious club our greatest gratitude. It had been no mere supplement to our gymnasium studies, if anything the reverse. The club was what had truly borne fruit—it had supplied the framework for our quest for education, and we had sketched our formal schooling into *it*.[15]

It was thanks to our club, we knew, that we basically never

thought about a so-called career back then. All too often, the state tries to exploit those years, luring civil servants it can make use of as early as possible and then securing their unconditional obedience with exaggeratedly strenuous exams,[16] but our method of self-cultivation had saved us. Practical concerns had not guided us; we felt no need to advance quickly and get on with our careers, so much so that neither of us yet had any idea what we wanted to be later, or worried about it in the least. A fact that seemed consoling, as we sat on our benches. Our club had nurtured this happy unconcern; if for nothing else, we gave thanks for that carefree spirit with all our heart, at this ceremony of ours. I have already said that, in the present day, it is almost impossible to believe that anyone could rock oneself in the cradle of the present, not goal-directed at all, content in the moment. If such a condition is possible, it must certainly be reprehensible. Our times are so averse to anything and everything useless, and how useless we were back then! How proud we were not to be of use! We could have competed for the honor of being the *most* useless. We did not want to be of any importance, represent anything, achieve anything; we wanted to be without a future, mere do-nothings lounging on the threshold of the present—and that's what we were, praise be to us![17]

—That is how it seemed to us at the time, honored listeners.—

Full of such solemn self-contemplation, I was more or less of a mind to answer the question about the future of our personal educational institution for myself, in the same self-satisfied tone, when the nature-music issuing from the philosopher's distant bench started to change in character. It grew gradually more insistent, more articulated. Suddenly I realized I could hear what they were saying, and that I was listening, that I was eagerly listening, all ears, as it were. I nudged my friend—perhaps he was dozing off—and whispered, "Wake up! There is something for us to learn here. What they're saying applies to us, even if it was not meant for us."

What I had heard was the philosopher's young companion defending himself, rather excitedly, while the philosopher attacked him in an ever more thundering tone of voice. "You haven't changed," he shouted. "Alas! You haven't changed! I can hardly believe how little difference there is in you between now and seven years ago, the last time I saw you, when with uncertain hopes I sent you on your way. Once again, and no pleasant task it is, I have to scrape off this modern veneer of education you have been coated with—and what do I find underneath? The same unchanging 'intelligible' nature, as Kant would say, but unfortunately an unchanged *intellectual* nature, too—the latter's immutability probably just as necessary, but less consoling.[18] What is the point of having spent my life as a philosopher, I wonder, if you—someone intelligent and truly eager to learn—could spend so many years with me without them making any real impression! You are acting as though you never heard the cardinal principle of education that I returned to again and again in our earlier discussions, so many times. Do you remember what it was?"

"I remember," the reprimanded student answered. "You always said that no one would strive for education if they knew how unbelievably small the number of truly educated people actually was, or ever could be. But that it was impossible to achieve even this small quota of truly educated people unless a great mass of people were tricked, seduced, into going against their nature and pursuing an education. As a result, we must never publicly betray the ridiculous disproportion between the number of truly educated people and the size of our monstrously overgrown educational system. That is the real secret of education, you said: Countless people fight for it, and think they are fighting for themselves, but at bottom it is only to make education possible for a very few."

"That's right," the philosopher said. "And yet you were capable of forgetting its true lesson, enough to believe that you were one of these few yourself? Because that is what you thought—I can tell. It's part and parcel of the worthless nature of our educated times. People democratize the rights of genius in order to avoid the true work of culture and demands of education. Anyone and everyone wants to lie back in the shadow of the tree that the genius has planted, while avoiding the hard necessity of working for that genius, of making him possible. You say you are too proud to want to be a teacher? You despise the crowd of students pressing in on you? You speak disparagingly of the teacher's task? And then, angrily defining yourself against that crowd, you want to lead a lonely, solitary life, imitating me and how I live? You think you can reach in a single bound what I have only managed to achieve at the end of a long and stubborn struggle to live as a philosopher? And you are not afraid that this solitude will have its revenge on you? Try to be a hermit of culture, just try it—to live for all, out of oneself alone, takes riches indeed! —Strange young men! Always thinking they have to imitate precisely what is highest and most difficult, what only a master can do, while they of all people should know how difficult and dangerous it is, and how many excellent talents might yet perish in the attempt!"

"I do not want to keep anything from you, teacher," his companion replied. "I have heard too much from you and spent too much time in your presence to devote myself body and soul to our current educational and pedagogical regime. I feel all too clearly its hopeless errors and defects, which you have so often pointed out—and yet I see in myself all too little of the strength I would need to prevail in a valiant struggle. I felt totally discouraged; my flight into solitude was not arrogance or presumption.

"Let me tell you what I think characterizes the vital and pressing educational and pedagogical questions of today. It seems to me we need to distinguish between two dominant tendencies in our educational institutions, apparently opposed but equally ruinous in effect and eventually converging in their end results. The first is the drive for the greatest possible *expansion* and *dissemination* of education; the other is the drive for the *narrowing* and *weakening* of education. For various reasons, education is supposed to reach the widest possible circle—such is the demand of the first tendency. But then the second tendency expects education to give up its own highest, noblest, loftiest claims and content itself with serving some other form of life, for instance, the state.[19]

"I think I know where the loudest and clearest call for the maximum expansion of education is coming from. Expansion is one of the favorite national-economic dogmas of the day.[20] As much knowledge and education as possible—leading to the greatest possible production and demand—leading to the greatest happiness: that's the formula. Here we have Utility as the goal and purpose of education, or more precisely Gain: the highest possible income. From this point of view, education essentially means acquiring the discernment that keeps a person 'up to date,' tells him all the ways to most easily make money, gives him power over the various channels along which individuals and peoples conduct their business. The true task of education, in this view, is to form people who are, as the French say, 'au courant'—the same way a coin is courant, valid currency. The more of these 'circulating' people there are, the happier the nation is as a whole. And that is the goal of the modern educational institution: to make everyone as 'current' as it lies in his nature to be, to train everyone to convert his innate capacity for knowledge and wisdom, whatever it might be, into as much happiness and income as possible. Everyone has to be able to give an exact appraisal of himself, has to determine exactly how much he has a right to demand from life. The 'link between intelligence and property' that this view alleges is practically an ethical demand. Those who hold this view hate any education that makes a person go his own way, or that suggests goals above and beyond earning money, or that takes a lot of time: They even try to dismiss these different educational ideas as 'higher egotism' or 'unethical educational epicureanism.' What the moral code operating here demands is the exact opposite: a *rapid* education, so that you can start earning money quickly, and at the same time a thorough enough education so that you can earn *lots* of money. Culture is tolerated only insofar as it serves the cause of earning money, but that much culture is also demanded. In short: humanity has a necessary claim to earthly happiness and that is why education is necessary—but that is the only reason why!"

"I would like to say something here," the philosopher said. "This perspective, which you have described so clearly, gives rise to a great, even monstrous danger: that at some point the masses will jump over the middle step and run straight after earthly happiness. This is what people today call the 'social question.' In other words, it may seem to these masses that education for the greatest number of people is merely a means to the earthly happiness of the few, and nothing more. Striving for 'universal education' weakens education so much that it can no longer bestow any privileges or be worthy of any respect at all. The most universal education of all is barbarism, is it not? But I do not want to interrupt your argument."

His companion went on: "Aside from this beloved national-economic doctrine, there are other motives for this expansion of education that we see so many people so valiantly advocate. There are countries where the fear of religious oppression is so widespread, and anxiety about the consequences of this oppression so pronounced, that people in every class of society thirst for education and gulp down whatever parts of education will dissolve the religious instincts. Elsewhere, it is occasionally the state that tries to promote as widespread an education as possible, in its own interest, since it feels strong enough to clamp back down on even the mightiest unleashing of education, and it has found again and again that a well-educated civil service or military helps it compete against other states. In this latter case, the foundation of the state has to be broad and firm enough to support the complex, delicately balanced arch of education; in the former case, the history of religious oppression must be tangible enough to necessitate so desperate a countermeasure. In short, whenever the masses sound the war cry of universal popular education, I try to decide whether it arises from a rampant drive to acquire possessions, the stigma of previous religious oppression, or the calculating self-interest of the state.

"On the other hand, I hear another tune being struck up from various sides, not as loud but at least as emphatic: that of the *narrowing of education*. People in any academic circle will hum a snatch of this tune in your ear: the universally acknowledged fact that the current system reduces scholars to being mere slaves of academic disciplines, making it a matter of chance, and increasingly unlikely, for any scholar to turn out truly *educated*. Academic study is spread across such a large area now that anyone with real but unexceptional talents and academic ambitions will devote himself to a narrowly specialized subfield, remaining totally unconcerned with everything else.[21] As a result, even if he stands above the vulgar masses within his subfield, he belongs fully with them in everything else—in everything important. A scholar with such a rarefied specialty is like a factory worker who spends his entire life doing nothing but making one single screw, or a handle for a given tool or machine, a task at which he will obviously become an incredible virtuoso. In Germany, where they know how to drape such painful facts in a glorious cloak of ideas, this narrow specialization among scholars, this straying ever farther from true education, is praised, even in moral terms: 'attention to detail' or 'industrious drudgery' is celebrated above all else, while lacking all culture outside one's own field is a badge of honor, a sign of noble moderation.[22]

"There have been centuries when it was self-evident that scholars were 'educated' and the educated were scholars. We would be hard-pressed to equate the two now, given the lessons of our time. The premise now accepted everywhere, and resisted nowhere, is that people should be exploited to serve science and scholarship.[23] Does anyone ask whether a scholarly discipline that consumes its creatures so vampirically is worth it? In practical terms, the academic division of labor is doing just what religions sometimes try to do: diminish education, even destroy it. For certain religions, given their origins and history, this may be a perfectly reasonable goal, but for scholarship it may well be suicidal. We are already at the point where the scientist or academic as such has nothing to say about any serious general question, especially the deepest philosophical problems, while a gluey mass that has worked its way into and between all the sciences—journalism—exists precisely to address such questions. Journalism fulfills its task according to its nature and as its name suggests: as day labor.

"It is in journalism that the two tendencies converge: education's expansion and its narrowing. The daily newspaper has effectively replaced education, and anyone who still lays claim to culture or education, even a scholar, typically relies on a sticky layer of journalism

—a substance as sturdy and permanent as the paper it's printed on—
to grout the gaps between every form of life, every social position,
every art, every science, every field. The newspaper epitomizes the
goal of today's educational system, just as the journalist, servant of
the present moment, has taken the place of the genius, our salvation
from the moment and leader for the ages.

"Now you tell me, my most excellent master, how I could hope to
fight the inversion and perversion of all true striving for education
that we now find dominant everywhere. How much courage can I,
as one lone teacher, have when I know full well that the steamroller
of pseudo-education will crush every seed of true education I cast?
Think how useless a teacher's greatest labors are now, when he tries
to lead one single student back to the infinitely distant and elusive
Hellenic world, the true homeland of our culture, and an hour later
that same student reaches for a newspaper or popular novel or one of
those scholarly books whose style bears the repulsive mark of today's
educational barbarism!"

"Enough!" the philosopher cried at this point, in a strong, sympathetic voice. "I understand you better now, and I should not have
spoken so harshly before. You are right about everything—except
your discouragement. Let me now tell you something that will give
you solace."

LECTURE II
February 6

HONORED listeners!

Those of you joining me today, having heard perhaps only rumors of the lecture I gave three weeks ago, must now permit me to bring you, without further ado, into the middle of a serious conversation in progress. I started to retell that conversation in my first lecture, and I will now remind you all of the last turn it had taken.

An important philosopher's younger companion had just explained to his teacher, in honest and forthright fashion, why he had become demoralized, left his teaching post, and was spending his days in inconsolable, self-imposed solitude. Arrogance had played no part in his decision.

"I have heard too much from you, teacher, and spent too much time in your presence," the worthy young man said, "to have faith in our current pedagogical and cultural regime. I feel all too clearly its hopeless errors and defects, which you have so often pointed out, and yet I see in myself all too little of the strength I would need to prevail in a valiant struggle to shatter the bulwarks of this supposed education. My flight into solitude was not arrogance or presumption; I felt totally discouraged." He then explained his actions by giving his view of the educational system in such a way that the philosopher could not help but respond in a sympathetic, reassuring tone. "You have said enough, my poor friend," he said. "I understand you better now, and I should not have spoken such hard words to you before. You are right about everything—except your discouragement. Let me now tell you something that will give you solace.

"How long do you think today's schools will persist in the educational practices that weigh so heavily upon you? I make no secret of what I think: Their time is past, their days are numbered. The first man who dares to be completely honest about them will hear his honesty echoing back from a thousand other brave souls. For buried in the men of the present age, beneath all their noble gifts and warm sentiments, is an unspoken common cause: every one of them remembers what he had to suffer in school; every one of them wants, if nothing else, to save his descendants from such a system, even at some risk to himself. But due to the sad poverty of spirit in pedagogy today, this longing is never voiced openly. There is no true creative talent here, which is to say truly practical men with good new ideas, who know that real genius and correct practice necessarily go together; our plodding practitioners have no good ideas, and thus no correct practice, either. Just read around in today's pedagogical literature—anyone not utterly horrified to see it clumsily chase its own tail with an incalculable poverty of spirit is beyond help. Here, our philosophy must begin not with wonder but with horror, and no one incapable of such a feeling should touch pedagogical matters. The reverse has been the rule up until now, of course. Those who were horrified, like you, my poor friend, ran skittishly away, while the reasonable types, not susceptible to horror, laid their coarse hands coarsely upon the most delicate process in any art: the process of education. But soon this state of affairs will no longer be possible. Let just one honest man turn up with good new ideas and the courage to bring them to fruition, even at the cost of breaking with everyone and everything around him; let him present just one glorious example, which coarse hands, the only ones hitherto at work, could never imitate; then people will begin to see and feel the difference, at least, and have a chance to reflect on the reason for it. They will no longer believe, as so many in all good conscience still do, that the craft of pedagogy can be the labor of coarse hands."

His companion replied, "Honored teacher, you give voice so courageously to your hopes: Give me an example, just one, if you can, to help me to share them. The gymnasium, for instance, which we both know well: Do you actually think that honesty and good new ideas can eradicate the stubborn old habits there? It seems to me that the gymnasium defends itself not with a hard wall, strong enough to withstand the battering ram, as it were, but with the deadly, slippery tenacity of all its principles. There is no tangible, visible opponent to crush, only a masked enemy able to take on a hundred shapes and slip free, giving way like a coward and then suddenly bouncing back to confound his attackers again and again. It was the state of the gymnasium, in particular, that made me flee into demoralized solitude, because I felt that if you could win that battle, all the other educational institutions would have to follow suit, but if you lost, there would be no choice but to give up on all the most serious pedagogical questions. So, master, instruct me: What hope can we cherish for the gymnasium's destruction, and its rebirth?"

"I, too, feel the gymnasium is as important as you say," the philosopher replied. "Every other institution is measured against its educational goals; any wrong turn the gymnasium takes will affect all the others. Renewing and purifying *it* will renew and purify the rest. Even the university can no longer claim such central, decisive importance—from at least one important angle, which I will clarify later, the university in its current form must be seen as merely an extension of the gymnasium.

"For now, let us consider why I am hopeful that one of two things must happen: either the spirit of the gymnasium as it has come down to us, motley and difficult to pin down as it is, will dissolve on its own into thin air, or else it will have to be purified and renewed from the ground up. So as not to overwhelm you with generalities, let me begin concretely with something we have all experienced in the gymnasium and all still suffer from. Scrutinized with a rigorous eye, what is *German class* at the gymnasium today?

"First, let me say what it should be. Everyone nowadays automatically speaks and writes in a German so vulgar and bad that it could only exist in an age of Newspaper German.[1] That is why any nobly endowed young man should be forcibly placed under a bell jar of good taste and strict linguistic discipline. If that is not possible, then better to return to speaking only Latin, out of shame at a language as ruined and debased as ours.

"What should the task of an institution of higher learning be, when it comes to language, if not to lead linguistically wild and unkempt youths to the right path, with dignified rigor and this authoritative command: 'Take your language seriously! If you cannot feel a sacred duty here, then you have not even the seed of higher culture within you. How you handle your mother tongue reveals how much you respect art, or how little; how close an affinity you have for it. If certain words and turns of phrase habitual in today's journalism do not inspire physical disgust, then abandon your pursuit of culture. Here, right before you, every time you speak and write, you have a touchstone for how difficult and enormous a task the cultured person faces today, and how unlikely it is that many of you will become truly educated.'

"Were this the gymnasium's command, the German teacher's duty would be to point out, with the complete assurance of a good ear, a thousand little details to his students and to categorically forbid them from using phrases such as 'to call for,' 'to pocket,' 'take into account,' 'seize the initiative,' 'it goes without saying,' and so on and so forth *cum taedio in infinitum*. This teacher would also have to show, line by line, how carefully and rigorously we would have to take every turn of phrase in our classic writers if we kept a true feeling for art in our hearts and the goal of complete intelligibility in our sights. He will force his students to express the same thought over and over again, a little better each time, and will stop at nothing until he has inspired in the less gifted students a pious awe for the language and in the more gifted a noble enthusiasm.

"Such is the task of so-called formal education—one of the most valuable tasks of all. But now what do we find at the site of this so-called formal education, the gymnasium of today? Any true judge of what goes on there will know what to make of these alleged educational institutions. Originally designed not to foster education and culture but to promote mere erudition,[2] they have recently turned their back on even that, and now aim at journalism. Nowhere is this more evident than in the teaching of German.

"Instead of providing purely practical instruction and accustoming the student to rigorous self-improvement through a strict cultivation of language, teachers everywhere take a scholarly historical approach to the mother tongue. They teach German like a dead language, with no sense of obligation toward its present and its future. This historicism has become so prevalent in our time that even the living body of our language is handed over for anatomical dissection. But education begins precisely when we understand that a living thing is *alive*; the task of the educator is precisely to *suppress* the 'historical interest' that presses in on all sides, especially where it is a question of *proper action,* not merely *understanding* something. Students need to learn how to use the mother tongue properly—and this practical perspective is the only justification for teaching German in our educational institutions. The historical approach seems much easier and more comfortable to the teacher, of course; it is appropriate even for the less talented and demands much less effort and will.[3] But what is easy and comfortable always cloaks itself in proud terminology and ostentatious pretentions—we see this in every pedagogical field. The practical approach appropriate to true education—the approach that actually works—is always fundamentally more difficult, and thus earns only looks of resentment and disdain. That is why the honest man has to make this *quid pro quo* clear, both to himself and to others.

"What motivation for studying the German language does the teacher typically offer, besides these scholarly considerations? What link does he forge between the spirit of his educational institution and the spirit of the *few* truly educated members of the German people, the classic poets and artists? This is a dark and dubious domain, and one must be brave indeed to shine a light into it, but we cannot refuse to look: someday everything, here too, will have to be made new. In today's gymnasiums, the still-unformed spirits of the students are stamped with the sickening features of our aesthetic journalism; the teacher himself sows the seeds of crude misunderstandings of our classic writers, a *desire* to misunderstand that will later blossom into what pretends to be aesthetic criticism but is actually nothing but insolent barbarism. Students learn to speak of our incomparable Schiller with schoolboyish superiority; they are taught to respond to his noblest and most German conceptions— the Marquis of Posa in *Don Carlos,* Max and Thekla in *Wallenstein* —with a supercilious smile that is an outrage to the German spirit, and which a better posterity will blush to recall.

"The third and last domain of the typical gymnasium German teacher—often considered the pinnacle of his activity, and sometimes even the pinnacle of gymnasium education altogether—is the so-called *German essay.* It is almost always the most gifted students who tackle this assignment with special pleasure, and that alone should make it clear how tempting and dangerous a task it presents. The essay appeals to the student's individuality; the more aware a student is of his distinguishing qualities, the more he gives his German essay a personal stamp. Most gymnasiums even require this 'personal stamp' through the choice of topics offered to students, and for me the strongest proof of this fact is that students in earlier grades are asked to describe their own life and development, an inherently unpedagogical topic. One need only peruse the lists of German essay topics across several gymnasiums to be convinced that the vast majority of students will probably, through no fault of their own, suffer for life from this work of individuality demanded too soon—this breeding of immature thoughts in their minds.[4] How often a whole literary career can seem like nothing more than the sad consequence of this pedagogical original sin against the spirit!

"Consider what happens when someone produces such an essay at that age. It is the first thing he writes on his own; his still-undeveloped powers coalesce and crystallize for the first time; the dizzying feeling of having been asked to be independent gives the result a magical halo of newness, destined never to return. All his natural audacity is called forth from the depths; all his vanity, unchecked by any stronger barrier, is for the first time permitted to take literary form. From that point on, the young person feels himself to be *finished*: feels able, indeed encouraged, to speak with anyone on equal terms. The topics assigned to him force him, in fact, to cast his vote on works of poetry, or lump together historical figures in a character sketch, or tackle serious ethical problems independently, or even turn the spotlight upon himself and portray his own development, delivering a critical report on his own self. In short, a whole world of deeply intellectual and self-reflective tasks is presented to a surprised young man who has had practically no self-awareness up until that point, and made a matter of his own judgment.

"Now think back to how teachers typically respond to these first original efforts, which do so much to shape the young student. What does the teacher deem worthy of criticism? What does he draw his student's attention to? Any extravagance of form or thought—which is to say, precisely what is typical at that age and particular to him. Any true independence the student may have, necessarily expressed in awkward, exaggerated, or grotesque form when provoked so prematurely—but still, this *is* the student's individuality—the teacher reprimands and rejects in favor of what is unoriginal, conformist, and respectable. Lockstep mediocrity receives tired, grudging praise, because the teacher finds himself bored by it, and with good reason.

"Perhaps there are others who see these essay assignments as the farce they are: not only the most absurd feature of the gymnasium today but also the most dangerous. The essays demand originality, but the only originality possible at that age is then rejected. They presuppose a formal education that only very few people will ever acquire, even in riper years. They treat every student as being capable of literature, as *allowed* to have opinions about the most serious people and things, whereas true education will strive with all its might precisely to *suppress* this ridiculous claim to independence of judgment on the part of the young person, imposing instead strict obedience to the scepter of the genius. They ask writers to present ideas in a larger framework, at an age when their every last written or spoken sentence is a barbaric abomination. And let us not forget how easy it is to awaken smug self-satisfaction during those years:

think of the vanity of the young man seeing his literary reflection in the mirror for the first time. Given all this, who could possibly doubt that the exercise stamps each rising generation with everything that ails our literary and artistic public sphere: the hasty overproduction driven by self-regard; the shameful churning out of books;[5] the complete lack of style; immature formulations that miserably sprawl or lack character altogether; the loss of any aesthetic canon; the reveling in anarchy and chaos; in short, the literary traits of our journalism, and no less of our scholars.

"So few people nowadays realize that one in a thousand, at most, is justified in putting his writing before the world. *Everyone* else who attempts it, at his own risk, earns as the just reward for every sentence he sees into print nothing but Homeric laughter from readers capable of true judgment—for truly, it is a spectacle for the gods, watching a literary Hephaestus limp up with his pathetic offerings. To inculcate serious and unrelenting critical habits and opinions is one of the highest tasks of formal education; the ubiquitous encouragement of everyone's so-called 'individual personality' is nothing but a mark of barbarity. But surely it is clear, from what I have said thus far, that German classes today are designed to foster 'individual personality,' not educate. And as long as gymnasiums continue to promote despicable, unconscionable scribbling by assigning German essays; as long as they refuse to take as their sacred duty the imposition of practical discipline on what is closest to hand, the spoken and written language; as long as they treat their mother tongue as nothing but a necessary evil or a dead body, I cannot consider them educational institutions in any true sense of the word.

"Above all, gymnasium language instruction shows no sign of being influenced by the *classical model*. This alone, to my mind, makes it dubious and misleading to claim that our gymnasiums provide a so-called 'classical education.' The tremendous seriousness with which the Greeks and Romans considered and handled their language, from youth on, is clear at a glance: This is what the classical Greek and Roman world is a model *for*—how could anyone fail to see it!—even if that world is held up as the highest and most instructive model for the gymnasium's educational program in other ways (although I, for one, have my doubts about that, too). The gymnasium's claim to sow the seeds of 'classical education' is really nothing but an embarrassed excuse, trotted out whenever anyone disputes its ability to instill culture. Classical education! That sounds so distinguished! It shames the attacker and slows the attack—for it takes time to get to the bottom of any phrase so distracting and disorienting.

"This is the gymnasium's habitual tactic: Depending on where the battle cry rings out from, it writes on its shield—not exactly covered with badges of honor—one of three confusing slogans: 'classical education,' 'formal education,' 'academic training.' Three glorious things, but unfortunately they are partly self-contradictory, partly contradicting each other. Violently yoking all three together can only produce some mythical educational tragelaphos: half stag, half goat. A truly 'classical education' is something so egregiously rare and difficult, demanding such a complex array of talents, that only the most naïve or shameless would hold it out as a goal that the gymnasium can achieve. The term 'formal education' is a piece of crude, unphilosophical phraseology that one must simply try to free oneself from, since there is no such thing as 'material education' standing in contrast to it. Finally, anyone who holds up 'academic training' as the goal of the gymnasium abandons then and there any 'classical education' or so-called 'formal education,' indeed abandons the gymnasium's whole educational mission, since the academic and the truly educated man of culture belong to two different spheres, which may occasionally overlap in a particular individual but which never coincide.[6]

"When we compare these three stated goals of the gymnasium with what we actually observe in German class, we can see what they primarily are in practice: embarrassed pretexts, evasive maneuvers for use in battle and war, which often work to bewilder the enemy. There is nothing in German instruction the least bit reminiscent of the grand ancient language training we call classical; German essays, as I've said, provide a formal education that turns out to be the absolutely arbitrary whim of 'individual personality,' or in other words anarchy and barbarism; and as for the academic training that is supposed to result from this instruction, let our German professors impartially judge how little the lifeblood of their discipline owes to these early scholarly efforts in the gymnasium, and how much it owes to the individual personalities of particular university instructors.

"In sum: The gymnasium has neglected and still neglects the one place where true education begins, and the readiest subject to hand: the mother tongue. As a result, the natural, fertile soil for any future educational process is missing. Only rigorously disciplined, artistically scrupulous linguistic standards can create a proper feeling for the greatness of our classical writers, but up to now gymnasiums have praised these classics only on the basis of the content of certain tragedies and novels, or because of various individual teachers' dubious aesthetic hobbyhorses. And yet one must know from personal experience how difficult language is; after searching long and struggling hard, one must reach on one's own the path our great poets stride, if one is to feel how lightly and gracefully they walk it and how stiffly and awkwardly others follow in their footsteps.

"After being subjected to such discipline, and only then, the young person will feel physical disgust for the 'refined diction' of our literati and the 'elegance' of style so beloved and praised in our novelists and mass-producers of journalism. He will be raised in a single stroke, once and for all, above a whole range of truly comical debates and scruples, for instance whether Auerbach[7] and Gutzkow[8] are great writers: He will simply be too disgusted to read them at all, problem solved. Let no one think it easy to develop one's sensitivity to the point of physical nausea—but let no one hope that it is possible to acquire an aesthetic sense along any other path except the thorny one of language, and by that I mean linguistic self-discipline, not linguistics.

"To make a serious effort here is to undergo an ordeal like that of a grown man becoming, say, a new soldier, who has to learn how to walk after having been merely a crude dilettante or empiricist of walking. These are laborious months. He is afraid he will tear a tendon; he loses all hope of ever being able to perform these artificial, consciously learned movements and place his feet easily and comfortably; he is shocked to see how awkwardly and crudely he actually puts one foot in front of the other; he worries he will entirely unlearn how to walk without ever learning to do it properly. But suddenly he realizes that these artificially drilled movements have turned into a habit, become second nature. All the certainty and power of his stride are returned to him, stronger than before and even with a certain grace. Now he, too, knows how hard it is to walk, and he has earned the right to mock the crude empiricists of walking, the dilettantes of walking with their pretense to elegance. Our 'elegant' writers have never learned to walk; their style proves it. Our gymnasiums do not teach this skill, either; our writers prove it. But a proper linguistic gait is the beginning of culture—and, if begun correctly, it eventually produces a physical sensitivity to 'elegant' writers that we call 'nausea.'

"We see here the fateful consequences of our gymnasium system. Gymnasiums cannot impart a true, rigorous education, which is above all obedience and habituation; at best they can only encourage and stimulate scholarly impulses. This explains the alliance we so often find between erudition and barbaric taste—between the academy and the newspaper. Scholars today, with a shocking lack of exceptions, have fallen away from, or shall I say sunk beneath, the educational heights that, thanks to the efforts of Goethe, Schiller, Lessing, and Winckelmann, the German system once reached. We see this falling away in the gross misunderstandings to which these great men are subjected, by literary historians (whether named Gervinus or Schmidt)[9] as much as by others—in practically any conversation, in fact, with 'educated' men and women.

"The clearest evidence of this decline, though, as well as the most painful, is the current state of pedagogical writing about the gymnasium. For half a century or more, this body of writing has not even mentioned, much less recognized, the only value such great men have for true educational institutions: their value as leaders and guides, pathbreaking mystagogues of classical education, with whom alone can be found the true path back to classical antiquity.

There is *only one* natural, healthy starting point for a so-called classical education: artistically serious, rigorous training in the use of the mother tongue. Almost no one finds this path and the secret of form alone, from within; everyone else needs great leaders and teachers and must trust their protection. But unless this sense of form is fully developed, there is no way for any classical education or culture to grow. The awakening of this sensibility, able to distinguish between form and abomination, is the first flutter of the wing that can carry us to the only true homeland of culture: Greek antiquity. That wing alone cannot bear us very far, of course, as we attempt to reach the infinitely distant stronghold of Hellenic culture, ringed round with its adamantine ramparts. We need these leaders, these teachers, our classic German writers, if we are to be borne aloft, under the wing-beats of their quest for antiquity, to the land of deepest longings: Greece.[10]

"Barely a whisper of this, the only possible relationship between our classic writers and classical education, has penetrated the antiquarian walls of the gymnasium, needless to say. Rather, our philologists indefatigably try to bring Homer and Sophocles to young souls unaided, and they call the result 'classical education,' a euphemism no one objects to. Let us each look to our own personal experience, and judge how much of Homer and Sophocles these tireless teachers have given us. We are here in the realm of the most prevalent yet most powerful delusions, of unintentionally spread misunderstandings. I have never once found in the German gymnasium a single gossamer thread of anything that can truly be called 'classical education,' and no wonder, given how the gymnasium has freed itself from the German classics and any German linguistic discipline. Classical antiquity cannot be reached by a blind leap into the void, and yet the whole treatment of ancient writers in our schools, all the righteous paraphrasing and commentating of our philological schoolmasters, is just such a leap into the void.

"A feeling for classical Hellenic culture is so rare a result, of artistic gifts together with the most strenuous educational struggle, that the gymnasium's claim to awaken it can only rest on a brutal misunderstanding. And awaken it in people of what age? Young enough to be blindly yanked around by the gaudiest fashions of the day; too young to have the slightest sense that *if* this feeling for the Hellenic ever should awaken, it could only express itself in a constant fight against the supposed culture of the present day. For today's gymnasium student, the Greeks as such are dead: He likes Homer just fine, but a novel by Spielhagen[11] is much more exciting; yes, he is happy to gulp down the Greek tragedies and comedies, but a real modern drama like Freytag's *The Journalists*[12] moves him in an altogether different way. He is inclined to speak of all ancient authors just like the aesthete Hermann Grimm,[13] who at one point, in a convoluted essay on the Venus de Milo, finally muses: 'What does the form of this goddess matter to me? What use to me are the thoughts it awakens in me? Orestes and Oedipus, Iphigenia and Antigone, what do they share with my heart?'—No, my dear gymnasium students, the Venus de Milo has nothing to do with you ... and just as little to do with your teacher!

"Such is the sad fate of the gymnasium today. This is its secret. Who will lead you to the homeland of culture when your guides are blind and yet pose as seers! Who among you will attain a true feeling for the sacred earnestness of art when you are spoiled with methods that encourage you to stutter on your own when you should be taught to speak, to pursue the beautiful on your own when you should be made to piously worship the artwork, to philosophize on your own when you should be forced to *listen* to the great thinkers. The consequence is to keep you forever distant from antiquity, mere slaves to the present.

"Still, the most salutary thing about the gymnasium as we know it today is that it takes the Greek and Latin languages seriously for years on end. Students learn respect for grammar and the dictionary, for a language fixed by rules; a mistake is a mistake, and one need not be put out at every moment by the claim that caprices and misdemeanors of grammar and spelling, like the ones we find in today's German style, can be justified. If only this respect for language were not floating in limbo—a purely theoretical burden, as it were, from which one is immediately released on returning to the mother tongue! But the teacher of Latin or Greek typically doesn't bother with his native language; from the start, he treats it as a place to relax after the rigorous discipline of Latin and Greek—a realm in which to indulge the lazy congeniality with which Germans tend to handle everything native to them. The splendid practice of translating from one language into another, so beneficial in stimulating an artistic sense for one's own language, is never applied with appropriate rigor and dignity to German itself, the undisciplined language where these qualities are needed most. And even these translation exercises are becoming less and less common: It is enough to *understand* the classical languages, one needn't bother to *speak* them.

"Here again we see the tendency to see the gymnasium as a scholarly institution, an illuminating contrast with its former serious aspiration to provide a humanities education.[14] It was in the age of our great poets, of the few truly cultured Germans we have ever had, that the marvelous Friedrich August Wolf channeled into the gymnasium the new classical spirit streaming through these men from Greece and Rome. His bold beginning enabled a new image of the gymnasium, not as a sort of nursery for cultivating academic research but as first and foremost a genuinely holy place consecrated to a higher and nobler education.[15]

"Various external measures seemed necessary and some crucial ones were successfully applied to the modern form of the gymnasium, with lasting effects—but the single most important thing failed to happen: consecrating the teachers themselves to this new spirit. As a result, the gymnasium's goal is now far removed from the humanities education that Wolf championed. The absolute value placed on erudition and academic education—which Wolf himself overcame—has once again, after a long and wearying battle, ousted the educational principle that Wolf brought in, and erudition maintains its sole authority, if not as openly as it did before, then in disguise, its face hidden. Moreover, what ultimately made it impossible to bring the gymnasium into the grand procession of classical education was the un-German, almost foreign or cosmopolitan, character of these educational efforts; the belief that we could pull the home soil out from under our feet and still stand firm; the insane idea that by denying the German spirit, the national spirit itself, we could leap directly into the distant Hellenic world.

"The truth, of course, is that one must know how to find this German spirit in its hiding places, whether under fashionable cloaks or heaps of rubble; one must love it enough not to be ashamed of even its vestigial form; above all, one must make sure not to confuse it with what these days goes around proudly calling itself 'contemporary German culture.' The German spirit is, if anything, inherently opposed to such 'culture,' and it has survived—admittedly under a rough exterior, and hardly in impressive form—largely in domains whose lack of culture 'the present day' likes to complain about. On the other hand, what presumes to pass for 'German culture' today is a cosmopolitan composite, having the same relation to the German spirit as a journalist to Schiller, as Meyerbeer[16] to Beethoven. This 'culture' is influenced most strongly by the culture of France, a civilization un-German in its deepest, most fundamental nature, which we Germans then ape without talent and in the most dubious taste. Such imitation gives a lying, hypocritical form to German society, media, art, and stylistics. Needless to say, the copy never attains the artistic perfection that the original, a civilization emerging organically from the essence of the Roman, has continued to achieve almost up to the present. To feel the contrast, one need only compare our most prestigious German novelists with any French or Italian novelist, even the less famous ones. Both sides share the same doubtful tendencies and aims, and the same still more dubious means. But there we find artistic seriousness, correctness of language at the very least, often joined with real beauty, and a harmony with corresponding social and cultural conditions throughout. Here everything is unoriginal, flabby, unpleasantly sprawling or lolling around in shabby house clothes of thought and expression, not to mention lacking any true social background—displays of erudition and academic mannerisms reminding us that in Germany it is the failed academic who becomes a journalist, while in the Latin countries it is the artistic, cultured person. The German can never expect to prevail with this allegedly German but fundamentally derivative culture: The French and the Italian will put him to shame and, when it comes to cleverly imitating a foreign culture, so too will the Russian.

"All the more firmly, then, do I cling to *the German spirit*, as revealed in the German Reformation[17] and in German music, and which, in the tremendous courage and rigor of German philosophy, in the recently tested loyalty of the German soldier,[18] has shown proof of that lasting strength averse to all false appearance. It is from this spirit that we, too, may expect to prevail over the fashionable pseudo-culture of 'the present day.' I hope that in the future schools will draw true culture into the battle and, especially in the gymnasium, inspire the younger generation with a burning passion for what is truly German. In doing so, schools will finally put so-called classical education on its natural footing once more and give it its only possible starting point. A true purification and renewal of the gymnasium can proceed only from a deep and violent purification and renewal of the German spirit.

"The link between the innermost essence of the German and the genius of the Greek is a mysterious bond, extremely difficult to grasp. But until the true German spirit, in its noblest and uttermost need, reaches out for the saving hand of Greek genius, as though for a firm handhold in the raging river of barbarism; until an all-consuming desire for what is Greek breaks forth from this German spirit; until the distant view of the Greek homeland, laboriously achieved, with which Schiller and Goethe refreshed their spirits, has become a place of pilgrimage for the best and most gifted among us—until then, the gymnasium's goal of classical education will flutter about in the air, untethered to anything. And those who work to nurture erudition in the gymnasium, however limited a form of academic spirit that might be, so as to have at least one real, firm, and in some sense ideal goal in view and save their students from the seductions of the glittering phantom now known as 'culture' and 'education'—they will have nothing to reproach themselves for. Such is the sad state the gymnasium finds itself in today: The narrowest, most limited points of view are in some sense correct, because no one is capable of reaching, or even pointing to, the place from which these views can be seen to be wrong."

"No one?" the philosopher's student asked, with no little emotion in his voice. And both men fell silent.

LECTURE III

February 27

Honored audience!

At the end of my last lecture, the conversation I had overheard and that remains fresh in my memory, whose basic lineaments I have tried to retrace for you here, was interrupted by a long and earnest pause. The philosopher and his companion, sunk in melancholy silence, felt the topic of their discussion—the crisis of the gymnasium, our most important educational institution—as a weight on their soul that no single individual, however well-intentioned, was strong enough to lift, and that the masses had no intention of even trying to lift.

Two things in particular grieved our solitary thinkers. First, that what would *rightly* be called "classical education" is nothing but a free-floating cultural ideal with no chance of taking root in the soil of our existing educational system, while what is *customarily* called "classical education"—with not a single voice raised in protest—is nothing but an aspirational illusion, which at best succeeds in keeping the phrase "classical education" alive, proving that it has not lost its solemn sound and pathos. Second, when it comes to the teaching of German, it was clear to these two honest men that the gymnasium of today had no idea how even to begin to build a higher education on the pillars of antiquity. The degenerate state of instruction in German, the intrusion of historical erudition in place of practical discipline and a training in good linguistic habits, the connection between certain gymnasium assignments and the regrettable spirit of our journalistic public sphere—all these clearly visible signs persuaded them that, sadly, not a trace remained of the beneficent powers emanating from classical antiquity, which could prepare students for their struggle against the barbarism of the present day and that might once again transform our gymnasiums into arsenals and armories for that struggle. On the contrary, the spirit of antiquity was being categorically rejected, even as the gymnasium gates were thrown wide open to what, mollycoddled by shameless flattery, passes for "contemporary German culture."

If our forlorn interlocutors felt any hope at all, it was that things must grow even worse before long—that what only a few had hitherto suspected would soon be urgently clear to the many, and that the time for honest and resolute men was close at hand, in the crucial realm of popular education, too.

"All the more firmly, then," the philosopher had said, "do I cling to *the German spirit*, as revealed in the German Reformation and in German music, and which, in the tremendous courage and rigor of German philosophy, in the recently tested loyalty of the German soldier, has shown proof of that lasting strength averse to all false appearance. It is from this spirit that we, too, may expect to prevail over the fashionable pseudo-culture of 'the present day.' I hope that in future the schools will draw true culture into the battle and, especially in the gymnasium, inspire the younger generation with a burning passion for what is truly German. In doing so, schools will finally put so-called classical education on its natural footing once more and give it its only possible starting point. A true purification and renewal of the gymnasium can proceed only from a deep and violent purification and renewal of the German spirit.

"The link between the innermost essence of the German and the genius of the Greek is a mysterious bond, extremely difficult to grasp. But until the true German spirit, in its noblest and uttermost need, reaches out for the saving hand of Greek genius, as though for a firm handhold in the raging river of barbarism; until an all-consuming desire for what is Greek breaks forth from this German spirit; until the distant view of the Greek homeland, laboriously achieved, with which Schiller and Goethe refreshed their spirits has become a place of pilgrimage for the best and most gifted among us—until then, the gymnasium's goal of classical education will flutter about in the air, untethered to anything. And those who work to nurture erudition in the gymnasium, however limited a form of academic spirit that might be, so as to have at least one real, firm, and in some sense ideal goal in view and thus save their students from the seductions of the glittering phantom now known as 'culture' and 'education'—they will have nothing to reproach themselves for."

After the two had reflected in silence for some time, the younger man turned to the old philosopher and said, "You have wanted to console me, teacher, and you have given me greater insight, and thus strength and courage. Truly, I look upon the battlefield more boldly now, and condemn my all too hasty retreat. We are not fighting for ourselves alone. We cannot and must not care how many will fall in the struggle, or whether we ourselves will perhaps be among the first to perish. Precisely because we are committed to the struggle, we need not give a thought to the poor individual; the moment one sinks to the ground, another will pick up the flag we have sworn to follow. Whether I have the strength for this struggle, whether I will hold out, no longer concerns me; to fall under the mocking laughter of the enemy may well be an honorable death, since, after all, their seriousness so often struck us as laughable. When I think of the way I and others in my generation prepared for the same career, the highest position a teacher can have, I realize how often we laughed at precisely the opposite things, and were serious about the most different things as well—"

"Now now, my friend," the philosopher interrupted with a laugh, "you are talking like someone who wants to jump into deep water without knowing how to swim, afraid not so much of drowning as of being laughed at for *not* drowning. But the last thing we should fear is being laughed at. There are so many truths to speak on this topic, so many frightening, embarrassing, unforgivable truths, that we will certainly not lack for enemies who sincerely hate us, and their rage alone will now and then produce an embarrassed laugh. Just think of the incalculable hordes of teachers who have cast their lot with the existing educational system, and who cheerfully, unreflectingly want to continue it. How do you think they will react when they hear about plans that exclude them, *beneficio naturae* no less;[1] or of demands that far exceed their middling abilities; or of hopes that find no echo in their hearts; or of struggles whose battle cry they cannot even begin to understand, and in which the only role they have to play is that of a dull, resistant, leaden mass?

"It is probably no exaggeration to say that the vast majority of teachers at institutions of higher education will find themselves in this position—hardly a surprise to anyone who considers how these people come into existence, how they *become* teachers of higher learning. Institutions of higher education have proliferated everywhere in such numbers that more and more teachers are needed to teach there: more than any population, even the most extravagantly talented, could possibly produce by natural means. As a result, far too many people with no true calling end up as teachers, and then, due to their overwhelming numbers and the instinct of *similis simili gaudet,*[2] they come to define the spirit of those institutions. Only someone without the slightest understanding of pedagogy could believe that laws or policies might somehow transform our undeniably excessive quantity of gymnasiums and teachers into an excess of quality, an *ubertas ingenii,*[3] without reducing their number. No, we must proclaim with one voice that people truly destined by nature for an educational path are infinitely few and far between, and that far fewer institutions of higher education than we have today would be enough to let these rare people develop successfully. In today's educational institutions, intended for the masses, precisely the people for whom such institutions should exist are the ones who receive the least support.

"And the same is true with respect to teachers. The best among them—the only ones worthy of the honorable title, if judged by a higher standard—are probably the least well suited to educate the young people who have been thrown together in the gymnasiums of today, not chosen for the path of education. In fact, such teachers must in a way keep hidden from their students the best they have to offer. Meanwhile, the overwhelming majority of teachers feels perfectly at home, because their limited gifts correspond and in a certain sense harmonize with the low level and inadequacy of their students. It is this majority that resoundingly calls for establishing more and more gymnasiums and institutions of higher learning.

"Indeed, we live in an age when the incessant, bewilderingly shifting call for education gives the impression that some tremendous cultural need is desperately thirsting to be satisfied. But it is just here that one must know how to listen properly—here, refusing to be led astray by the ringing sound of these educational slogans, is where one must take a straight, hard look at those who talk so tirelessly about the cultural demands of the age. One will then feel a strange disappointment, my dear friend; we have felt it often. These heralds proclaiming the needs of culture, seen from up close, appear suddenly transformed into eager, even fanatical enemies of true culture—one that holds firm to the aristocratic nature of the spirit. Their fundamental goal is the emancipation of the masses from the rule of the great individuals. What they are working toward is the overthrow of the most sacred order in the empire of the intellect: the servitude, submissive obedience, and instinctive loyalty of the masses to the scepter of genius.[4]

"I have long since grown accustomed to looking hard at the eager advocates of so-called 'popular education' as it is commonly understood.[5] Most of the time, what they consciously or unconsciously want is unfettered freedom for themselves in a universal saturnalia of barbarism. But the sacred natural order will never grant it to them: They are born to serve, to obey. Every time their creeping thoughts try to get anywhere on their wooden legs or broken wings, it only confirms the kind of clay from which Nature has made them, the mark with which she has stamped them. Education for the masses cannot be our goal—only the cultivation of the chosen individual, equipped to produce great and lasting works. We know full well, do we not, that a just posterity will judge the overall cultural condition of a people solely and entirely on the basis of the great heroes of the age, who stride in solitude; it will render its verdict based on how these heroes have been recognized, encouraged, and honored—or else pushed aside, mishandled, and destroyed. The people are given 'culture' in only a crude and completely external way when that is the direct goal, for example with mandatory universal primary education. The deeper regions where the masses come into true contact with culture—where a people harbors its religious instincts, where it continues to create its mythical images, where it stays faithful to its customs, its law, its native soil—are hardly ever reached along a direct path, and always through destructive violence. Truly advancing the cause of popular education in these serious realms means defending against such destructive forces while preserving the beneficent unconsciousness, the healthy sleep of the people, without which counterweight and remedy no culture, with the all-consuming tension and excitement it produces, can endure.

"But I know what those who want to interrupt the beneficent, healthy sleep of the people really want. They constantly cry to the people: 'Wake up! Become conscious! Be smart!'—and even as they pretend that the extraordinary increase in the number of schools, and the creation of a proud class of teachers in consequence, satisfies a powerful need for education, I know their real goal. They are fighting, and this is how they fight, against the natural hierarchy in the empire of the intellect; they seek to destroy the roots of the highest and noblest cultural powers that, bursting forth from the popular unconscious, have a maternal destiny: to give birth to, raise, and nurture genius.

"Only with this metaphor of the mother can we grasp the importance of true popular education and its duty to the genius. The genius is not actually born of culture, or education: His origin is, as it were, metaphysical—his homeland metaphysical. But for him to appear, to emerge from a people; to reflect as it were in its full array of colors the whole image of a people and its strengths; to reveal this people's highest purpose in the symbolic essence of one individual and his enduring work, thereby linking his people to the eternal and liberating his people from the ever-changing sphere of the momentary—all of this the genius can do only if he has been ripened in the womb and nourished in the lap of his people's culture. Without this sheltering, incubating home, there is no way for the genius ever to unfold his wings and take eternal flight. Instead he sadly, swiftly steals away like a stranger driven forth from an uninhabitable country into wintry desolation."

"Teacher," his companion said, "you amaze me with this metaphysics of genius, and I have only a dim sense of the truth in these metaphors. But I understand perfectly what you said before, about the excessive number of gymnasiums and the resulting excess of teachers. My own experience convinces me that the overwhelming number of teachers who have basically nothing to do with education or culture, and have ended up on this path, with these pretensions, solely because of a demand for instructors, *must* be what determines the orientation of the gymnasium today. Once someone has experienced the shining moment of insight that reveals how unique and unapproachably remote Hellenic antiquity is, and has fought a difficult inner battle to defend this belief, he knows full well that this insight will always remain inaccessible to the many. Such a person will find it absurd, even undignified, to use the Greeks for, let us say, professional reasons—to earn his bread shamelessly prodding and poking around at this sanctuary with a workingman's hands and everyday tools. And yet this crude and disrespectful sensibility is universal in precisely the group of people who make up the majority of gymnasium teachers: the philologists.[6] So the fact that gymnasiums preserve and propagate this attitude comes as no surprise.

"Just look at the younger generation of philologists: How rarely among them do we see any sense of shame, any sense that we have no right to exist at all in light of a world like that of the Greeks. How cool, how brazen this young brood is, building its miserable nest in among the most magnificent temples![7] Smug and unashamed, they have been wandering around in that world's astonishing ruins since their university years; to the vast majority of them, a mighty voice should boom out from every corner: 'Away from here, uninitiates, you who will never be initiates! Fly without a word from this sanctuary, silent and ashamed!' Alas, such a voice would sound in vain—for even to understand such a Greek style of curse and anathema, you need a little of the Greek within you, while these people are so barbaric that they simply set up shop amid the ruins as comfortably as you please, bringing along all their modern pursuits and conveniences and tucking them behind the columns and funerary monuments. Then there is great rejoicing when they find in these ancient surroundings what they themselves have smuggled in.

"One of them writes poetry, and is clever enough to look up words in Hesychius's dictionary:[8] He is convinced at once that his calling is to modernize Aeschylus, and then he finds people gullible enough to claim that he and Aeschylus are *congenial*—he, a poetasting criminal! Another, with the suspicious eye of a police inspector, hunts down every contradiction, every hint of a contradiction, that Homer is guilty of: he wastes his life shredding and sewing back together the Homeric rags that he himself first tore off the magnificent original garment.[9] A third feels unsettled by antiquity's orgies and mysteries: He decides once and for all that only enlightened Apollo counts, and sees in the Athenian nothing but a cheerful, commonsense Apollinian, if somewhat immoral. What a sigh of relief he breathes when he has restored another dark corner of antiquity to his own level of enlightenment—when he discovers in old Pythagoras, for example, a sturdy fellow traveler in his enlightening politics. A fourth torments himself with the question of why Oedipus was condemned by fate to such abominable things—having to kill his father! and marry his mother! What was Oedipus guilty of? Where is the poetic justice? Suddenly he realizes the truth: Oedipus was actually a creature of passion, lacking all Christian charity. He even flew into an unseemly rage once, when Tiresias called him a monster and the curse of his country.[10] Be meek and gentle! Maybe that was Sophocles's lesson—otherwise you will be doomed to marry your mother and kill your father! Still others spend their whole lives counting the lines and syllables of the Greek and Roman poets and delighting in the proportion 7:13 = 14:26. Finally, someone announces that he has solved the Homeric question from the standpoint of prepositions, and thinks he can draw truth up out of the well with ἀνά and κατά.[11] All of these people, whatever they are doing, are rooting and rummaging around in the Greek soil so rest-lessly, so clumsily, that any true friend of antiquity cannot help but be troubled.

"If it were up to me, I would take by the hand anyone who feels the slightest professional inclination toward the ancient world, tal-ented or talentless, and declaim: 'Do you have any idea of the dan-gers that threaten you, young man, sent forth on your journey with nothing more than a little book learning? Have you heard that, ac-cording to Aristotle, being crushed by a falling statue is not a tragic death?[12] This is just the death that threatens you! Are you surprised? You should know that philologists have spent centuries trying to raise once more the statue of Greek antiquity, long since fallen and sunk into the earth—and they have never succeeded, for it is a colos-sus, on which any individual can only clamber around like a dwarf. Tremendous collective efforts, all the leverage of modern culture, have been brought to bear, and again and again this statue, barely raised from the ground, has fallen back to crush those beneath it.[13] And let it be so—every creature has to die of something. But who can ensure that the statue itself will not break! Philologists perish and are reduced to dust because of the Greeks—that is a loss we can live with—but for Antiquity itself to be shattered because of the philologists! Consider this, reckless young man, and withdraw, as-suming you are no iconoclast!'"

The philosopher laughed. "The truth is, many philologists nowa-days have indeed followed your call and retreated. This is very differ-ent from my experience as a young man. Today, whether consciously or unconsciously, philologists have largely come to the conclusion that any direct contact with classical antiquity on their part is point-less and hopeless. Even they consider such studies sterile, derivative, and obsolete. All the more happily, then, does this horde fall back on linguistics: an endless expanse of freshly cleared arable land where even the most limited minds can now find useful employment, where the very modesty of their ambition is considered a positive virtue, for a rank-and-file piece of work is exactly what is most de-sired, given the uncertainty of the new methods and the continuous risk of fantastical missteps. Here, no majestic voice resounds from the ruined world of antiquity to rebuff the newcomer. All who approach are welcomed with open arms; even someone on whom Sophocles and Aristophanes have never made any particular impression, in whom these writers have never once produced a creditable thought, even he can be set down before an etymological spinning wheel or sent out to collect the detritus of far-flung dialects, and so his day passes, linking and separating, gathering and scattering, running about in the field and consulting reference books in the study.

"But now this useful researcher is supposed to teach! He of all people, because of the work he has done in linguistics, supposedly has something to offer gymnasium students about the very same ancient authors who have never made the least impression on him, much less brought him any insight! It's a quandary all right. Antiquity has nothing to say to him, and as a result, he has nothing to say about antiquity. Suddenly a light dawns, and he feels better: Is he not a scholar of languages? And did these authors not write in Greek and Latin? Now he can cheerfully launch into etymologies, starting with Homer, and call on Lithuanian or Church Slavonic for help, and above all holy Sanskrit—as though Greek class were nothing but a pretext for a general introduction to linguistics, and as though Homer had just one main flaw: not having written in Proto-Indo-European.[14] Anyone familiar with today's gymnasiums will acknowledge how far removed their teachers are from any classical inclinations, and how, precisely because they are aware of this failing, the scholarly pursuit of comparative linguistics has gained such an upper hand."

"To me," the younger man replied, "it seems that the real problem is that the teacher of classical culture *doesn't* mix his Greeks and Romans with other, barbaric peoples—for him, Greek or Latin can *never* be just one language alongside others. Given his classicizing inclinations, it is completely irrelevant whether the languages are related, whether the skeleton of this language corresponds to the structure of that. Correspondence is not the point. Insofar as he teaches culture and tries to model himself on the noble classical prototype, he cares about what is *not in common*: the nonbarbaric qualities that set the Greeks and Romans apart and above all others."

"And maybe I'm wrong," the philosopher said, "but I suspect that mastery of language, the ability to express oneself comfortably in speech and in writing, is precisely what is being lost with how Latin and Greek are taught at gymnasiums today. My own generation, admittedly old now and much reduced in number, excelled at this ability; today's teachers, it seems to me, proceed with their students so textually and historically that at best they might turn out some more little Sanskritists, or etymological Roman candles, or wanton conjectural text reconstructors, but not a single student who can read his Plato or his Tacitus with pleasure, as we old men could. The gymnasiums may still be academic greenhouses, but not for a kind of scholarship that is the natural and unintentional offshoot, as it were, of an education with truly noble goals. They breed a scholarship comparable to the hypertrophied swelling of an unhealthy body. Scholarly obesity is what the gymnasium-nurseries of today produce, if indeed they have not degenerated into wrestling schools for the elegant barbarism that nowadays fancies itself 'contemporary German culture.'"

"But where," his companion replied, "should these countless poor teachers go, with no dowry of natural talent to bring to true culture and offering their services as teachers only out of necessity, since they need to put food on the table and since a surplus of schools requires a surplus of teachers? Where should they flee when antiquity imperiously rejects them? Must they not then fall victim to the forces of the present age that, day after day, call out to them through the indefatigably resounding organ of the press: 'We are culture! We are education! We are the pinnacle! We are the tip of the pyramid! We are the apex of world history!' They hear these seductive promises. But what they are told to embrace as the foundation of a totally new and superlatively advanced form of culture consists, in reality, of the most ignominious symptoms of anticulture, the plebian 'culture pages' of magazines and newspapers! If even the barest suspicion survives in them that these promises are lies, then where should these poor creatures go? Where else but into the stupidest, most pedantic, barren academic scholarship,[15] if only so as not to have to hear any more of this endless, indefatigable screeching for culture. Hounded this way, must they not finally stick their head in the sand like an ostrich? Is that not true happiness for them, to lead the underground life of an ant, buried under dialects, etymologies, and conjectures, miles away from true culture, but at least with their ears sealed shut, deaf and immune to the siren song of the elegant 'culture' of today?"

"You are right, my friend," the philosopher said. "But where is it written in stone that there have to be so many schools, and hence ever more teachers? After all, we are well aware that the demand for more schools comes from a sphere inimical to true education, and that it results in nothing but anti-education. There is only one reason why we think of this demand as written in stone: The modern state is in the habit of making its views on these matters known and accompanying its educational demands with saber rattling. This phenomenon naturally makes as strong an impression on most people as the voice of eternal truth written in stone, the primal law of things. Incidentally, the state that makes these demands—the 'culture state,' as they put it these days—is a recent development;[16] it has become 'self-evident' only in the last fifty years, a period when so many things have come to seem, to use the era's favorite word again, 'self-evident,' without for all that being evident in the least.

"The most powerful of these modern states, Prussia, is so bold and aggressive and at the same time so heavy-handed in its centralized management of culture and schooling that the dubious principle it has seized upon has become generally dangerous and a particular threat to the true German spirit. Systematic efforts are instituted to make sure that the gymnasium 'keeps up with the times,' as they say; measures to send as many students as possible to gymnasiums are encouraged, and in fact, the state here makes use of its most powerful inducement—the granting of privileges connected to military service—with such success that, according to the independent testimony of official statisticians, the general overcrowding of Prussian gymnasiums and the urgent, continual need to establish more of them can be traced back to this policy alone. How better to ensure an excess of educational institutions than by linking to the gymnasium every higher and most of the lower positions in the civil service, admission to university, and the most influential military positions with all their perks? In a country, moreover, where the bureaucracy's unbounded political ambitions and the widespread popular support for universal military service automatically pull anyone with any talent toward these spheres. The gymnasium is seen as first and foremost a step on the ladder of honor, a track that anyone who feels driven toward the sphere of government must pursue. This is a new phenomenon, or at least a peculiar one: the state itself acting as a mystagogue of culture. It advances its own aims by forcing every one of its servants to show his face only with the torch of general state education in hand, and by that flickering light he is meant to recognize the state as the highest goal, in fact the reward, of all his educational pursuits. Now this last point should really make these people stop and think. It should remind them, for instance, of a certain related tendency that only slowly came to be understood, a philosophy that was once promoted for the state's sake and to advance the state's aims: Hegelian philosophy. It would perhaps be no exaggeration to say that Prussia, by subordinating all educational aspirations to state purposes, has succeeded in appropriating the one legacy of Hegelian philosophy that can be exploited in practice: its apotheosis of the state, which, it must be said, reaches its pinnacle precisely through this subordination of education."

"But what can the state want from such a strange practice?" the philosopher's companion asked. "It must have some purpose—as we can see merely from how other states marvel at Prussian schools, study them carefully, and sometimes try to copy them. Clearly, other states see these schools as useful for a state's longevity and power, much like the famous universal military service that is now so widely adopted. In Prussia, where everyone wears the soldier's uniform with pride for a time, and practically everyone has acquired the state's cultural uniform, as it were, through the gymnasium, an enthusiast might almost be moved to speak of classical conditions: a state omnipotence, only ever achieved in antiquity, that almost every young man is driven by instinct and training to feel as the flower, the highest purpose, of human existence."

"Such a comparison," the philosopher said, "would indeed be an enthusiast's hyperbole, limping along on more than one lame leg. For this utilitarian perspective, in which culture deserves respect only insofar as it concretely serves the state, and in which any impulses that cannot immediately be adapted to the state's own ends should be stamped out, is as alien to the ancient state as can be imagined. That is precisely why the profound Greek felt an admiration for and gratitude to the state that would seem almost shockingly strong to modern people: He recognized that not a single seed of culture could grow and develop without the state's necessary protection; that his whole inimitable culture, unique in all of history, could flourish as luxuriantly as it did only under the wise and careful aegis of *these* protective institutions. The state was not the culture's border patrol and regulator, its watchman and warden, but the culture's sturdy, muscular, battle-ready comrade and companion, escorting his admired, nobler, and so to speak transcendent friend through harsh reality and earning that friend's gratitude in return. When the state lays claim to our enthusiastic gratitude nowadays, in contrast, it is surely not due to any chivalrous regard for German higher culture and art. In this regard, Germany's past is no less disgraceful than its present, as the slightest glance at how our great poets and artists are celebrated in German cities, and how these masters' artistic projects are supported by the state, will show.

"There must be some explanation, then, both for the state's tendency to promote everything here called 'culture,' and for the pseudo-culture it actually promotes, one which bows to the authority of the state. This tendency finds itself at war, open or concealed, with both the genuine German spirit and any culture or education that can be derived from it—as I have sketched out with hesitant strokes for you here, my friend. The idea of education promoted and encouraged with such intense interest by the state, and due to which its schools are so admired abroad, must therefore be rooted in a sphere that never touches the genuine German spirit—the spirit that speaks to us so wonderfully from the innermost core of the German Reformation, German music, and German philosophy. Like a prince in exile, this spirit is viewed with indifference and scorn by an education system wallowing in state sponsorship; this spirit is a stranger, wandering past in solitary grief, while pseudo-culture swings its censer back and forth, having arrogated to itself *its* name and *its* worth, playing a humiliating game with the word 'German' to the cheers of 'cultured' schoolteachers and journalistic scribblers.

"Why does the state need such a surplus of educational institutions and teachers? Why promote national education and popular enlightenment on such scale? Because the genuine German spirit is so hated—because they fear the aristocratic nature of true education and culture—because they are determined to drive the few that are great into self-imposed exile, so that a pretension to culture can be implanted and cultivated in the many—because they want to avoid the hard and rigorous discipline of the great leader, and convince the masses that they can find the path themselves...under the guiding star of the state! Now that is something new: the state as the guiding star of culture!

"Meanwhile, one thing consoles me. The German spirit, embattled as it is, and for which they have substituted such a gaudy stand-in—this spirit is brave. It will fight its way into a purer age and save itself. Noble as it is, and victorious as it will be, it will maintain a certain sympathetic attitude toward the state, even if the state, beleaguered and harried, allies itself with pseudo-culture. After all, what do we know of how difficult it is to rule over men: to preserve law, order, peace, and prosperity among millions and millions of people—who, to judge by the great majority, are boundlessly selfish, unjust, unreasonable, dishonest, envious, malicious, meanspirited, and at the same time thoroughly narrow-minded and perverse—while constantly struggling to protect what little the state has acquired for itself from covetous neighbors and treacherous thieves?

Under such pressures, a state naturally turns to any ally it can, and when one of these allies goes so far as to offer its services with pompous phrases—when it describes the state, in Hegel's words, as an 'absolutely perfected ethical organism,' and holds up as the task of education the job of discovering where and how a person can best serve state interests—how surprising is it that the state then falls into the arms of such an ally, crying out with full conviction, in its deep, barbaric voice: 'Yes! You are education! You are culture!'"

LECTURE IV
March 5

HONORED listeners!

Having loyally followed my story up to this point—now that we have made it this far through a lonely, remote, occasionally rude dialogue between a philosopher and his companion—you are now, I can only hope, inclined to make your way like hale and hearty swimmers through the second half of our journey, especially since I can promise you that a few more puppets will soon appear in the little marionette theater of my narrative, and that, in general, if you have persevered until now, the waves of the story will carry you more quickly and easily to its conclusion. What I mean to say is that we have almost reached a turning point—and so it is all the more appropriate to take a short look back and recall what we may have gathered from this wide-ranging conversation.

"Remain at your post!" the philosopher appeared to be exhorting his companion. "You are right to hope! For it is ever more obvious that we have no educational institutions, and that we need them. The gymnasium was established for this noble purpose, but our gymnasiums are either hothouses of a dubious 'culture' that seeks to defend itself against a true education it truly hates (that is, an aristocratic education limited to a few select individual souls), or else the breeding grounds of a small-minded, sterile, academic erudition that may serve to make us deaf and blind to the blandishments of that dubious 'culture,' but that has nothing in common with education." The philosopher had drawn his companion's particular attention to the strange degradation that is inevitably at the heart of a culture whenever the state believes it controls culture and can pursue state aims by means of culture; whenever the state enlists culture in the struggle against foreign enemies as well as what the philosopher dared to call the "truly German spirit." This spirit—whose noblest needs link it to the spirit of the Greeks, which has proven steadfast and courageous in the difficult past, pure and lofty in its aims, and which can, through its art, respond to the highest calling, that of freeing modern man from the curse of modernity—this spirit, the philosopher said, is condemned to live in isolation, cut off from its legacy. Yet its slow lament, echoing through the wasteland of the present, terrifies the cluttered and gaudily bespangled cultural caravans of our time. We *should* provoke terror, the philosopher said, not just wonder; we must attack, he advised, not timidly flee; above all, he encouraged his companion not to worry too much about the individuals whose higher instincts fill them with revulsion against the barbarism of the present day. "Let such a one perish: the Pythian God was not unwilling to find a new tripod, a second Pythia, so long as the mystic vapor still welled up from the deep."

Once again the philosopher intoned: "Note well, my friend, two things that must never be mistaken for each other. A person needs to learn much if he is to live, to fight his battle for survival—but everything he learns and does with that aim, as an individual, has *nothing* to do with education and culture. On the contrary, culture begins in a layer of the atmosphere far above the world of necessity, scarcity, and struggle. The question is how much a person values himself over and against other individuals, how much of his strength he decides to expend in the personal struggle for survival. Some, by stoically restricting their needs, rise up quickly and easily into the sphere in which they can forget and as it were shake off their own selfhood, enjoying eternal youth in a solar system of timeless, impersonal concerns. Others enlarge their subjective needs and sphere of influence to construct a mausoleum of astounding size for themselves, as if they could thereby defeat that monstrous adversary, time. In this impulse we likewise see a longing for immortality: riches, power, intelligence, quickness of mind, eloquence, a healthy appearance, a famous name—all these are merely means by which the insatiable personal life force yearns for new life, thirsts for an ultimately illusory immortality.

"But even in this highest form of subjectivity, with the maximal needs of a broadened and as it were collective individuality, the needy self has no point of contact with true culture and education. And when such an individual craves *art* as well, it is only for art's power to stimulate or distract, the aspects of art that have the least connection to the pure and sublime, and the greatest to what is degraded and polluted. In all his actions and efforts—however splendid they may appear to others—this individual is never free of restless, desiring selfhood. The illuminated, ethereal space of selfless contemplation flees from him. Therefore, study and travel and collect though he may, he will live his whole life eternally distant, indeed banished, from true culture. For true culture disdains the pollution of the needy desiring individual; it wisely shuns all who try to use it as a means to their egotistical ends; when anyone thinks he can possess it, can use it to satisfy his needs and earn his living, it vanishes with silent footsteps and a mocking glance.

"So, my friend, you must not confuse culture—that pampered, tenderfooted, ethereal goddess—with the useful handmaiden who nowadays goes by that name, a mere intellectual servant and sometime adviser in matters of poverty, earning one's keep, and the necessities of life. No course of instruction that ends in a career, in breadwinning, leads to culture or true education in our sense; it merely shows how one can save and secure the self in the struggle for survival. This is what matters most to the vast majority of people, of course, and the more difficult the struggle, the more they must study and work hard while young. But let no one consider institutions that encourage and enable such people to carry on the struggle as educational institutions in any serious sense. Whether they claim to create civil servants or shopkeepers or soldiers or businessmen or farmers or doctors or engineers, they are teaching how to win the battle for survival. Their laws and standards must be very different from those of true educational institutions—what may be permitted, or even demanded, in one place may well be sacrilegious injustice in the other.

"Let me give you an example, my friend. If you want to lead a young person onto the right educational path, you will make sure not to disturb his naïvely trusting, direct and personal relationship to nature. Forest and stone, the storm, the vulture, the single flower, butterfly and meadow and mountainside must speak to him in their own tongue—he must be able to see himself in them as though in countless mirrors and reflections, in a colorful whirlpool of ever-changing appearances, and he will unconsciously feel the metaphysical oneness of all things in the great symbol of Nature, while also drawing peace from its eternal perseverance and necessity. But how many young people can be permitted to grow up like this, so close to nature, in an almost personal relationship with it? Most must learn a different truth, and learn it early: how to place nature under their yoke. The naïve metaphysics comes to an end; botany, zoology, geology, and inorganic chemistry force an entirely different view of nature onto young men. What is lost as a result of this compulsory new view is not some poetical phantasmagoria but the one true, instinctive understanding of nature; what takes its place is clever calculation and the drive to outwit and defeat nature. Only the truly educated person is granted the priceless treasure of being allowed to remain faithful to the contemplative instincts of his childhood, and so he attains a peace, unity, communion, and harmony that those raised for the struggle for survival cannot even dream of.

"So, my friend, do not think I want to withhold from our *Realschulen* and higher *Bürgerschulen* the praise they deserve.[1] I honor the places where children are taught math, master everyday commercial language, take geography seriously, and arm themselves with the astonishing discoveries of natural science. I am also more than willing to admit that students prepared by our better *Realschulen* are perfectly entitled to the same privileges as our gymnasium graduates, and it will surely not be long before universities and state offices are opened without restriction to students of these schools, as up to now they have been only to gymnasium students. Mind you, I mean entitled to the same privileges as the students of our gymnasiums today! I cannot fail to add this painful afterthought: If it is true that the *Realschule* and the gymnasium are now nearly identical in their aims, with only the slightest difference between them, so that they deserve equal recognition from the state, then that means another kind of institution is sorely lacking—that of true education! I do not in the least mean this as a criticism of the *Realschulen*, which have fulfilled their much lower but utterly necessary purposes with admirable honesty and success; but there is much less honesty in the realm of the gymnasiums, and much less success, too. There we see something like an instinctive feeling of shame, an unconscious recognition of the fact that the whole institution is miserably degraded, and that the barbaric desolation and sterile reality of the place refute the sonorous educational words of the clever apologists who teach there. There *are* no true educational institutions! And in the sham institutions that try to counterfeit culture and education, people are more hopeless, atrophied, and dissatisfied than by the hearths of so-called 'realism'![2] Incidentally, my friend, you can see how crude and uninformed this group of teachers is, if they are capable of misunderstanding the rigorous philosophical terms 'real' and 'realism' so completely that they suspect behind them an opposition between matter and spirit, and interpret 'realism' as 'being oriented toward the recognition, formation, and mastery of actual reality.' . . .

"As far as I am concerned, there is only one true opposition: between *institutions of education* and *institutions for the struggle to survive*. Everything that exists today falls into the latter category, but what I am describing is the former."

Perhaps two hours had passed while the philosophical companions were discussing these strange and troubling matters. Night had fallen, and if the philosopher's voice had already resounded like a kind of natural music in the twilit clearing, now, in the total darkness of night, whenever raised in excitement or indeed passion, it broke in manifold thunders, blasts, and hisses against the tree trunks and cliffs falling off into the valley. Suddenly he fell silent. He had just repeated the almost plaintive phrase "We have no educational institutions, we have no educational institutions!" when something fell to the ground right in front of him—maybe a pinecone—and his dog leaped upon whatever it was, barking loudly. Interrupted by the noise, the philosopher raised his head and suddenly felt the night, the coolness, the solitude. "Well now, what are we doing here?" he asked his companion. "It has grown dark. You know who we're waiting for, but he won't come now. We have stayed late for nothing. We should go."

And now, honored listeners, it is time to tell you how my friend and I felt in our hiding place as we listened to this conversation, which we heard so clearly and followed so eagerly. I have already told you that we had decided to perform a kind of commemorative cere-mony there that evening—to honor nothing less than the cultural and educational riches we youthfully believed we had happily har-vested in our own lives thus far. We were especially grateful for an institution we had dreamed up on this very spot some years before: a small circle of companions devoted to encouraging while also monitoring our vital cultural urges, as I have already described. Now, as we eavesdropped in silence and abandoned ourselves to the philosopher's strong words, an entirely unexpected light had been shined upon our whole past. We felt like people who are absent-mindedly strolling around and suddenly see an abyss at their feet: not only had we failed to avoid the greatest danger, we were actually running right toward it. Here, at the very place we honored so deeply, we heard the warning cry: "Back! Not one step farther! Do you know where your feet are carrying you, where this glittering path is tempting you to go?"

Now, it seemed, we did know, and a feeling of overwhelming gratitude drew us so powerfully to this loyal Eckhart[3] with his seri-ous warnings that we both leaped up to embrace him. But we unex-pectedly rushed toward him just when he had turned to go, and his dog leaped up at us, barking loudly. The philosopher and his com-panion must have thought they were being ambushed by highway-men rather than about to be warmly embraced. Clearly, the philosopher had forgotten all about us. In short, he ran off.

We caught up with him, only to have our efforts to embrace him end in complete failure. At that very moment my friend screamed, bitten by the dog, and the philosopher's companion fell upon me with such force that we both tumbled to the ground. A strange and horrible tussle in the dirt ensued between man and dog, lasting several moments—until my friend managed to cry out in a loud voice, parodying the philosopher's words: "In the name of everything cultural and pseudo-cultural! What is this stupid dog doing here? Away, damned cur, uninitiated and never to be initiated! Away from us and our innards, too! Retreat in silence, silence and shame!"

After this speech, the situation became as clear as it could be in the total darkness of the forest. "It's you!" the philosopher cried. "Our young marksmen! What a shock you gave us! What made you dart out at me like that in the dead of night?"

"Happiness, gratitude, and respect!" we said, shaking the old man's hand while his dog let out a series of suspicious barks. "We could not let you leave without telling you how we felt. And you cannot leave yet, we have so much to explain, so many questions still to ask you about matters close to our hearts. Stay, stay—we will lead you down the mountain later, we know every step of the way perfectly. Maybe the visitor you are waiting for will still come. Look, down at the Rhine: what is that, swimming so brightly, as though in the light of many torches? I am looking for your friend there; I have a feeling that he will be coming up here with all those torches."

We besieged the astonished old man with our requests, our promises, and our fantastical suggestions, until finally his companion persuaded him to walk back and forth on the mountain a little longer, in the mild night air. "Unburdened of all the smoke of knowledge," he added.

"Shame on you!" the philosopher said. "Whenever any of you wants to quote something, you can't come out with anything but *Faust*. But all right, I agree, with or without your quotation—as long as our young men here hold their ground and don't run off as suddenly as they arrived. Such will-o'-the-wisps! You're amazed when they're there and amazed again when they're not."

At this point, my friend immediately recited:

> Out of reverence, I hope, we should succeed
> In forcing easygoing Nature.
> Our path is usually only zigzag.[4]

The philosopher marveled and stood there. "You surprise me," he said, "my esteemed will-o'-the-wisps. This is no swamp! Where do you think you are? What does it mean to you to be near a philosopher? The air is clear and sharp, the soil dry and hard. You will need to find a more fantastical region if you want to zig-zag."

"I think these gentlemen have already told us," the philosopher's companion put in, "that a vow compels them to stay here for the time being. But it also strikes me that they have listened to our comedy of education as the chorus, in fact as truly 'ideal spectators,'[5] since they did not bother us, and we did not even know they were there."

"Yes, that is true," the philosopher said. "We cannot deny you this praise, but it seems to me that you have earned praise even greater—"

Here I clasped the philosopher's hand and said, "Only someone as brutish as a reptile, lying on the ground, head in the mud, could hear speeches like yours and not become serious, thoughtful—and feel a thrill of enthusiasm. Perhaps what you say would make some people angry, from chagrin or self-accusation, but the impression it made on us was different. I don't know how to describe it. We had chosen this exact place and time; we were in such a receptive mood; we sat there ready, like open vases—and now I feel filled to overflowing with this new wisdom, because I am absolutely at my wit's end. If someone asked me what I plan to do tomorrow, or for the rest of my life, I would have no idea how to answer. Clearly, we have lived and pursued education in entirely the wrong way until now—but what should we do to cross the chasm that separates today from tomorrow?"

"Yes," my friend agreed, "that's how I feel, too. I have the same question. But then it starts to seem that such a noble, idealized view of the task of German education and culture can only scare me off... Am I worthy to take part in this project? I see a glittering procession of the most richly endowed natures approaching the goal, and now I have some idea of the abysses the procession must pass over, the temptations it must avoid. Who would be so bold as to join this procession himself?"

Here the philosopher's companion turned to him as well and said, "Please don't be angry with me if I tell you I feel much the same way. Talking to you, I often feel raised up high above my level and warmed by your courage, your hope—I forget who I am. Then comes a sobering moment, the biting wind of reality brings me back to my senses, and I see only the chasm that lies between us, across which you had been carrying me as in a dream. Your vision of education hangs on me, or rather weighs heavily on my breast, like a crushing coat of chain mail; it is a sword I am not strong enough to swing."

Suddenly the three of us stood united before the philosopher. Mutually encouraging and prodding one another, pacing slowly back and forth on the treeless plateau that had served as our shooting range earlier that day, in the utterly silent night under a calm starry sky spread out over our heads, we spoke more or less as follows: "You have said so much about the genius and his solitary, difficult wandering through the world, as though nature were capable of producing only polar opposites: on the one hand, the stupid, sleeping masses who proliferate by instinct alone, and on the other, enormously distant from them, the great contemplative individuals who are capable of eternal creations. But you yourself call these individuals the top of the intellectual pyramid: don't there logically have to be countless intermediate levels between the broad base with its heavy burden and the pinnacle soaring free into the air? Here, if nowhere else, the saying *natura non facit saltus* must apply.[6] Where does what you call culture begin—which block of stone marks the boundary between the lower sphere and the higher? And if we can truly speak of 'culture' only with respect to these most distant beings, how could their incalculable nature be the basis of an institution—what would it even mean to imagine educational institutions that benefit solely these chosen few? They are precisely the ones who know how to find their path already, it seems to us. Their ability to stride undisturbed through the buffets and blows of world history, like a ghost moving through a crowded gathering, without the educational crutches that everyone else needs to walk with—that is just what reveals their power."

Together we said something along these lines, in an awkward jumble; the philosopher's companion went further and said, "Think of all the great geniuses we are proud of—the ones we call the genuine leaders and pathfinders for the true German spirit, whose memories we honor with statues and celebrations, whose works we confidently hold up to other nations. Where did they find an education of the kind you call for? To what extent were they nourished and ripened in the sun of a native education? And yet, it was possible for them to exist; they became what we now hold in such high esteem; their works might even be said to justify the process of formation they went through, including the lack of education that we would probably have to say characterized their era and people. What did Lessing[7] or Winckelmann[8] need from a German education? Nothing—or at least no more than Beethoven, Schiller, Goethe, all our great artists and writers. Maybe it is simply a law of nature that only posterity can recognize the heavenly gifts which give an earlier age its excellence."

At this point the old philosopher could no longer contain his rage. "Oh, you innocent lamb," he screamed at his companion, "bleating of the simplicity of knowledge! Oh, nothing but suckling baby animals, the lot of you! What skewed, bumbling, cramped, humpbacked, crippled arguments! I hear in them the sound of today's education; my ears are ringing with sheer 'self-evident' historical facts and relentlessly sophomoric historical rationalizations! Remember this moment, oh undefiled Nature—you are old, this starry sky has hung above you for thousands of years, but never before have you heard such educated and fundamentally wicked empty talk as the beloved chitchat of the present age!

"So, my good Teutons, you are proud of your poets and artists? You point to them and brag about them to foreign nations? And since it cost you no effort to have them here among you, you spin the delightful theory that there is no reason to take any trouble about them in the future, either? They come all by themselves, isn't that right, my innocent children? The stork brings them! Let's not even talk about midwives! Well now, my good men, you need a serious lesson. You think you can feel proud that these brilliant, noble spirits whose names you invoke were smothered, exhausted, and prematurely snuffed out thanks to you and your barbarism? You can think without shame of Lessing, reduced to dust by your idiocy, the conflict with your ludicrous totems and idols,[9] the wretched state of your theaters, your scholars, your theologians—Lessing, never once able to venture that eternal flight for which he had come into the world? And what do you feel when you remember Winckelmann, who, to free himself from the sight of your grotesque absurdities, went begging for help to the Jesuits and whose shameful religious conversion dishonors not him but you? Do you dare speak Schiller's name without blushing? Look at his picture! The flashing eyes that gaze contemptuously out over your heads, the deathly flushed cheeks—do they say nothing to you? Here was a glorious plaything of the gods, and you broke it. If not for Goethe's friendship, his mortally harassed and curtailed existence would have been snuffed out even sooner by the likes of you![10] Not one of our great geniuses has ever received any assistance from you, and now you want to make it a dogma that none shall receive any in future? To each of them, you were that 'resistance of the obtuse world' of which Goethe speaks in his 'Epilogue to the Bell';[11] to each you showed a peevish lack of understanding, or narrow-minded envy, or malicious egotism; it was in spite of you that they created their immortal works, against you that they directed their attacks, and thanks to you that they died too soon, their work unfinished, bewildered and broken by the struggle. Who can imagine what these heroic men might have accomplished if the true German spirit had been able to spread its sheltering roof above their heads in the form of strong institutions?—the spirit that, without such institutions, drags out its isolated, ruined, degenerate existence. All those men were destroyed, and only a belief in the rationality of everything that happens, taken to the point of insanity, could absolve you of your guilt.

"And not they alone! From every realm of intellectual distinction accusers step forth to indict you. Whether I look at writers or philosophers or painters or sculptors—and not only those with the greatest gifts—I see nothing but talents immature, overexcited, prematurely exhausted, scorched or frozen before they came to fruition, and everywhere I feel that 'resistance of the obtuse world' of which *you* are guilty. That is what I mean when I demand true educational institutions and denounce as pitiful the places that go by that name today. Anyone pleased to call this demand 'idealistic,' or indeed related to any 'ideal' at all, no doubt hoping to fob me off with some kind of compliment, deserves the answer that what we have at present is simply villainous and disgraceful. Someone freezing in a barren wasteland who demands warmth will practically go out of his mind if he is accused of being 'idealistic.' It is a matter of clear and present, obvious, pressing realities: Anyone with any feeling for the issue knows that this is a real need, as real as cold or hunger. But if someone feels nothing—well, at least he now has a yardstick with which to measure where what I call 'culture' stops and which block of stone in the pyramid separates the lower realm from the higher."

The philosopher seemed in a kind of frenzy. He had stopped in his tracks and given this speech by the dead tree trunk that had earlier served as the target for our shooting practice; we urged him to walk on with us a little farther. Not a word was spoken among us for some time. Slowly and thoughtfully, we paced back and forth. Having put forward such foolish arguments, we felt not so much shame as a certain restoration of personality: After the philosopher's heated and not exactly flattering speech, we felt closer to him than before. I would go so far as to say we felt a more personal connection.

For such a miserable creature is man that nothing brings him closer to another more quickly than when the latter reveals a flaw, shows a sign of weakness. Our philosopher losing control of himself, heaping abuse on us, helped to bridge the gap that our timid respect, which was all we had felt for him up until then, had created. To anyone who finds such an observation shocking, let me add that this bridge can often lead from distant hero worship to personal love and sympathy; as we felt our personality restored, this sympathy began to come more to the forefront. Why were we leading this old man around at night, among rocks and trees? Since he had yielded to our pleas, why could the three of us not have found a humbler, gentler way to ask for instruction? Why did we have to contradict him, and with such clumsy words?

For now we realized how foolish, naïve, and incoherent our objections were, and how strongly the echo of the present resounded in them—the very sound the old man hated to hear in the realm of education and culture. Moreover, our objections had hardly been purely intellectual: What had provoked our resistance to the philosopher's speech apparently lay elsewhere. Maybe what had spoken from our mouths was only our instinctive fear that a man like him might not see us in a positive light; maybe all our earlier ideas now simply compelled us to reject his view, since his view completely rejected our own claim to culture and education. But one shouldn't argue with anyone who takes an argument personally—or rather, as the moral would go in our case: Anyone who takes an argument personally shouldn't argue, shouldn't contradict others.

So on we walked at the philosopher's side: sorry, ashamed, dissatisfied with ourselves, and more than ever convinced that the old man must be right and we had done him wrong. How far in the past our youthful dream of an educational institution now seemed—how clearly we recognized the danger we had avoided by sheer chance: that we might give ourselves up, body and soul, to the educational system that had called out to us so temptingly from the gymnasium, ever since our boyhood years. Why, in fact, had we not joined the public chorus of its admirers? Perhaps only because we were still real students, because we could still step back from the pushing and grabbing, could still retreat from the ceaselessly tumbling and crashing waves of public life onto our own little island—which now was about to be washed away as well!

Overwhelmed with such thoughts, we were about to say something to the philosopher when suddenly he turned to us and spoke in a gentler voice: "I have no right to be surprised if you young men act rashly and recklessly. For you can hardly have ever given serious thought to what you just heard me say. Give yourselves some time; take what I have said and carry it with you, think about it day and night. You now stand at a crossroads—now you know where the two paths lead. Follow the one, and your era will welcome you with open arms. You will not lack for honors and decorations; an enormous crowd will carry you along, with as many like-minded people thronging behind you as surging ahead. When the person up front gives the word, that word will echo through every rank and file. And on this path, the first duty is to fight in rank and file; the second duty, to take anyone who does not want to stand in rank and file and destroy him.

"On the other path, you will find very few fellow wanderers. It is a steeper, more winding, more difficult road, and those on the first path will mock you because your progress here is so much more laborious. They will no doubt also try to tempt you over to join them. And whenever the two paths cross, you will either be mistreated and pushed aside, or feared and shunned.

"Now what do the followers of these two paths, different as they are, understand by 'educational institution'? The enormous swarm thronging toward its goal on the first path takes the term to mean an institution that organizes them into rank and file, and excludes and expels anyone who in any way strives after higher and more distant goals. Naturally this horde knows how to use splendid words to describe their aims: For example, they will talk about the 'universal development of the individual personality within fixed, shared, national, common human principles,' or else proclaim their goal to be 'the foundation of a people's republic grounded in reason, culture, and justice.'

"For the second, smaller troop, an educational institution is something completely different. Those in this group want a solid structure to serve as a bulwark against the swarm of the first group, which wants to overrun them and separate them from their comrades; they want something to prevent any isolated individual from losing sight of his sublime and noble task through premature exhaustion, or by being diverted, corrupted, or destroyed. For them, the point of a common institution is to help the individual complete his work—but this work is as it were purified of every trace of selfhood, meant to rise above the ever-changing transience of the age and purely reflect the eternal, unchanging nature of things. The individuals in this institution, purified of selfhood, too, will also make every effort to prepare the way for the birth of the genius and the creation of *his* work. There will be many well suited to play such supporting roles, even among those whose gifts are of the second or third rank, and only by working in true educational institutions like these will they feel they are fulfilling their duty in life.

"These days, however, the continual seductions of fashionable 'culture' divert just such people with just such talents from their true path, leaving them adrift and cut off from their own instincts. Temptations assail their egotistical impulses, weakness, and vanity—the zeitgeist practically whispers in their ears: 'Follow me! There, on that path, you are servants, assistants, tools, outshined by higher natures, never free to enjoy your own individuality; you are yanked around on strings, cast in chains, like slaves, like machines! Here, with me, you will be in complete control of your own individual personality; your gifts will shine forth in their own right, bringing you—you!—into the first rank. Enormous crowds of followers will surround you; the acclaim of public opinion will gratify you far more than an aristocratically bestowed word of praise from the genius on high.' Today even the best of men succumb to such temptations, and in truth, what makes the difference cannot be said to be either the actual talent the person has or his receptivity to these voices, but a certain moral loftiness, an instinct for heroism and self-sacrifice, and, ultimately, a bedrock need for culture, initiated by proper education—which is first and foremost, as I have said, obedience and submission to the discipline of genius—and grown into a kind of moral requirement.

"But the so-called 'educational institutions' of our time know essentially nothing of this discipline, this submission, even though I have no doubt that the gymnasium was originally meant to foster true education, or at least to prepare students to receive it, and that in the wonderful, profoundly impassioned period of the Reformation they really did take the first bold steps along such a path. In the era of our Goethe and Schiller, too, we again see something of that need, so disgracefully diverted and hidden away, which like the first budding of the wing Plato speaks of in the *Phaedrus* bears the soul aloft toward the realm of the immutable pure Forms of things at every contact with the beautiful."

The philosopher's companion spoke up: "Ah, honored and most excellent teacher, now that you have invoked the divine Plato and the world of Ideas, I can no longer believe you are truly angry with me, no matter how much I may have earned your anger and disapproval with what I said earlier. As soon as you start to speak, I feel that Platonic wing stirring in me, and only when you fall silent do I, the charioteer of my soul, have trouble handling the resistant, wild, and unruly horse that Plato described as well: a crooked, lumbering animal put together any which way, with a short, thick neck, flat-faced, dark in color, with gray, bloodshot eyes, shag-eared and deaf, always ready for mischief and disrespect, and hardly yielding to whip or spur.

"Remember, too, how long I have lived apart from you, and that I too have been the target of all the seductive arts you describe. I may not even have realized it, but perhaps they were not entirely unsuccessful. I now understand more clearly than ever how important it is to have an institution that makes it possible to live among the rare men of true culture—to have them as our leaders and guiding stars. How dangerous it is to wander in solitude! When I thought I could flee to save myself from direct contact with the bustling spirit of the times, as I put it to you before, this flight was a sham. The atmosphere of the present continually soaks into us through countless capillaries, with our every breath, and no solitude is lonely and distant enough to put us out of reach of its clouds and fogs. The images of that so-called culture slink around us in ever-changing disguises—as doubt, as profit, as hope, as virtue—and even here, with you, having been taken in hand as it were by a true solitary champion of culture, this charlatanry has the power to mislead us. How steadfast and true, ever on the alert, the little troop of an almost sectarian culture must be! How they must support and strengthen one another! How rigorously they must scold every misstep, and how sympathetically forgive it! Teacher, having rebuked me so forcefully, please also forgive me!"

"You speak in a language I do not like, my good friend," the philosopher replied. "It reminds me of a religious conventicle. I want nothing to do with such things. But I liked that Platonic horse of yours, and I will forgive you for his sake. I'll trade you my suckling lamb for your horse.

"But I am not in the mood to keep walking out in the cold with you anymore. The friend I was waiting for may be foolish enough to come up here at midnight, since he promised to come, but I have waited in vain for the signal we agreed on, and I can't understand what could have kept him away so long. He is usually punctual and precise, as we old men are wont to be, something you young men tend to consider old-fashioned. But today he has left me in the lurch: How annoying! Well, come with me, it is time to go."

—Just then, something happened.

LECTURE V
March 23

Honored listeners!

If what I have told you thus far, of a philosopher's more or less violently agitated speeches delivered in the hush of night, has been heard with any sympathy, then the ill-humored decision I described at the end of my last lecture must have struck you much as it did my friend and me. He suddenly announced that he wanted to leave. His friend had stood him up; what we and his companion could offer him in this wilderness instead was not particularly enlivening; having stayed on the mountaintop longer than there was any reason to stay, he now wanted to leave quickly. He must have felt that the day was wasted; he no doubt wanted to put it behind him, casting off any memory of meeting us. And so, against our will, he insisted it was time for us to go, when something unexpected brought him to a standstill. His already upraised foot sank hesitantly back down to the ground.

We saw a colored glow from the direction of the Rhine, heard a loud crackling noise that quickly died out, and then, from the distance, a slow melodic phrase, sung in unison, many voices strong. "His signal!" the philosopher cried. "My friend is coming after all— I have not waited in vain! It will be a midnight meeting... But how can I let him know that I am still here? Come! Marksmen, now is the time to display your arts. Do you hear the strict rhythm of the melody that salutes us? Listen, and repeat it with your gunshots!"

Now this was a task to our taste and something we could actually do! We loaded as quickly as we could, conferred briefly, and raised our pistols toward the starlit peaks, while down in the valley the penetrating series of notes echoed and died away. One, two, three, our shots pierced the night—and then the philosopher shrieked, "Wrong rhythm!" For we had failed in our task. A shooting star had hurtled down, quick as an arrow, after our third shot and our fourth and fifth were fired at the same time, almost involuntarily, in the direction of its fall.

"Wrong rhythm!" the philosopher shrieked. "Who told you to shoot at a falling star? It can fall perfectly well without you! If you're going to handle weapons, you need to know want you're doing."

Just then, the melody from before rose up from the Rhine again, louder this time, intoned by more voices. "They understood anyway," my friend laughed, "and besides, who could hold his fire when such a bright apparition comes into range?"

"Be quiet!" the philosopher's companion interrupted. "What kind of mob is that, singing the signal? Twenty to forty voices, I would guess—strong, male voices. And where are they singing from? They don't seem to have left the far bank of the Rhine, so we should be able to see them from our side. Come, quick!"

We had been walking on the plateau near the massive dead tree, and our view of the Rhine was blocked by a thick, tall, dark woods. As I have mentioned, though, we could see through the treetops from a quiet little clearing not far downhill: the Rhine, with the island of Nonnenwörth cradled in its arm, lay as if in an oval frame. We hurried eagerly, though with all due consideration for the old philosopher, toward this quiet spot; it was pitch-black in the woods, and, leading the philosopher from either side, we could hardly see the trail but somehow divined it.

No sooner had we reached the benches in the clearing than we saw a large, dull, fiery, shifting glow, clearly from the other side of the Rhine. "Those are torches," I cried. "Surely those are my comrades from Bonn, and your friend must be in their midst. It is they who are accompanying your friend and who sang that song. Look! Listen! They are getting in their boats now; the torchlight procession will arrive up here in barely half an hour."

The philosopher leaped back. "What are you saying?" he burst out. "Your comrades from Bonn—students—my friend came here with *students*?"

This question, asked in something close to fury, angered us. "What do you have against students?" we countered, but we received no answer. Only after some time did the philosopher start to speak again, slowly and plaintively, as though to the one who had not yet arrived: "So, my friend, even at midnight, even on this lonely mountain, we will not be alone. You are bringing a band of troublemaking students up here, though you know full well that I much prefer to avoid that *genus omne*.[1] What do you mean by this, my distant friend? I do not understand. Our plans to meet again after so long apart, and here, in this remote place, at this unusual time—does that mean nothing to you? Why would we want a chorus of witnesses, and such witnesses! No sentimental, softhearted need brings us together: We have both long since learned how to live alone, in dignified isolation. It was not for our own sakes that we decided to meet here; not to nourish tender feelings or the like; not to stage a grandiloquent scene of friendship. No, here, where in a memorable hour I once met you in solemn solitude, we intended to give each other the most serious counsel, like knights of a new Vehmic court.[2] Let those who can understand us hear what we have to say—but why bring a mob of people who surely cannot understand us? It doesn't seem like you, my distant friend!"

It did not feel right to interrupt this bad-tempered complaint, and when the philosopher lapsed into gloomy silence, we did not have the courage to tell him how much his dismissive condemnation of students had naturally upset us.

Finally the philosopher's companion turned to him and said, "I am reminded, teacher, that back before I knew you, you too lived at various universities. Tales of your teaching methods and interactions with students are still going around. But from the resignation with which you spoke of students just now, one would think your experiences there must have been strange and upsetting. I suspect that you saw and experienced what everyone sees and experiences there, and simply judged it more severely, and rightly so. I have learned this much from the time I have spent with you: The most remarkable, instructive, decisive experiences in life are the everyday ones; the enormous riddle before everyone's eyes is precisely what almost no one sees as such. These problems are left untouched, in the middle of the sidewalk as it were, under the feet of the passing crowd—for the few true philosophers, who carefully pick them up, hold them high, and make them shine as precious gems of wisdom.

"Perhaps, in the time we have before your friend arrives, you can tell us a little about what you learned in the world of the university? That would bring our discussion of current educational institutions, and the observations we have unwillingly been forced to make, full circle. Let me remind you that you promised to do this, earlier this evening. You began by affirming the extraordinary importance of the gymnasium: Every other institution must be judged by its standard, however defined, and if the gymnasium goes astray then every other institution will suffer along with it. Universities, then, cannot claim to be the defining center of the system in the current model: At least from one important point of view, they are merely an extension of the gymnasium. You promised you would make this argument in detail later—as perhaps our student friends here might be able to attest, if they happened to hear that part of our conversation."

"Yes, we heard that," I said.

The philosopher turned to us: "Well then, if you really were listening closely, why don't you tell me what *you* see as the mission of the gymnasium today, after everything I have said. Furthermore, you are still close enough to that realm to judge my thoughts on the basis of your own experience and impressions."

My friend, in his quick and nimble fashion, replied as follows: "Up until now, we have always believed that the purpose of the gymnasium was to prepare students for the university. This preparation was meant to make us independent enough to enjoy the extraordinary freedom of a university student—for no one in any sphere of life today is given as much freedom of choice and action as a student, it seems to me.[3] He has to be his own guide for several years, across a

wide plain left entirely open to him. The gymnasium, then, is supposed to make him independent and self-sufficient."

I continued my friend's speech: "In fact, it seems to me that everything you criticize the gymnasium for—and I'm sure you're
right—is needed to foster a kind of independence in students, or at
least their belief that they are independent. That is the intended purpose of the German essays you talked about earlier: The individual
must learn to delight in having his own goals and views of his own,
so that he can walk without crutches later. That is why he is encouraged to produce work so early, and criticism and sharp judgments
earlier still. Even if Latin and Greek cannot inspire in students a
passion for distant antiquity, then at least the current method of instruction can awaken scholarly feelings, a desire for strictly causal
knowledge, a passion to uncover and discover. How many students
have been seduced once and for all by the charms of academic scholarship because they found in the gymnasium a new way of reading
and caught it in their young fingers! The gymnasium student has to
study all sorts of things, gather all kinds of knowledge, and this
probably, little by little, creates in him a drive to study and gather in
the same way at the university, on his own. In other words, the mission of the gymnasium, in our view, is to prepare students to live and
study independently, the same way they were forced to live and study
under the gymnasium system."

The philosopher laughed at this, but not entirely good-naturedly.
"And what a fine example of independence you have given me here!
Just the independence I find so shocking, and which makes it so un-
pleasant to be around today's students. Yes, my good friends, you are
prepared, you are mature, you are complete—Nature broke the
mold after she made you, and your teachers have every right to re-
joice in your existence. What freedom, certainty, and aplomb your
judgments show! How new and fresh your insights are! You sit in
judgment, and every culture of every age scatters before you; your
scholarly feelings are kindled, and fire shoots from your fingers—
look out, everyone, make sure you don't get burned! And your professors, I see they are no less independent—they take independence

to an even more forceful and charming level. Never was an era so rich in magnificent independences, and never has slavery of any kind been so hated—including, of course, the slavery of education and culture!

"Permit me, though, to judge this independence of yours by that standard—the standard of true education and culture—and let us see how your universities measure up. When someone from abroad wants to learn more about our university system, his first pressing question is: How are your students connected to the university? We answer: Through the ear—they take part in university life as listeners. The foreigner is amazed and asks: Purely by listening? Purely by listening, we repeat. The student attends lectures. Insofar as he speaks, or sees, or walks, or spends time in others' company, or makes art—insofar as he lives and breathes, in short—he is independent, that is to say, not dependent on the educational institution.[4] Now it very often happens that the student writes something down while he is listening. These are the moments when he is attached to the university by a kind of umbilical cord. He can choose what he wants to hear; he does not necessarily have to believe what he hears; he can shut his ears if he does not want to hear at all. This is the 'acroamatic' method of instruction.[5]

"The teacher, then, speaks to these listening students. Anything else he may think or do remains inaccessible to them, cut off by a monstrous chasm. He often reads while he speaks. In general, he wants as many listeners in attendance as possible, but if need be, he makes do with a few, almost never with just one. One speaking mouth plus many ears and half as many writing hands: that is the academic system as seen from the outside—the educational machinery of the university in action. And the possessor of this mouth is separated from, and independent of, the possessors of those many ears.

"This double independence is glorified as 'academic freedom.'[6] To make for even greater freedom, the one can say whatever he wants, more or less, and the other can listen to whatever on offer he wants, more or less—except that in the background, a discreet distance away from both parties, the state stands watching with a certain supervisory look on its face, making sure to remind everybody from time to time that *it* is the aim, the purpose, the essence of this whole strange process of speaking and listening.[7]

"We, who must be permitted to regard this astonishing phenomenon solely as an educational institution, will then inform the inquiring foreigner that what our universities call 'education' and 'culture' passes from mouth to ear, and that any instruction is merely, as I have said, 'acroamatic.' But since the listening, even the choice of what is to be listened to, is a matter of the independent-minded student's personal judgment, and since this student can refuse to believe anything he hears, can deny it all authority, the educational process is strictly speaking left in the student's own hands. The independence that gymnasiums aspired to produce now struts about proud as can be in its most brilliant plumage, presenting itself as 'independent higher education.'

"Oh happy age, when the young are wise and educated enough to teach *themselves* how to walk![8] Oh incomparable gymnasiums, cultivating independence while other eras believed in cultivating dependence, discipline, subordination, and obedience—resisting with all their might every delusion of independence! Now, my good friends, do you see why, from the standpoint of education, I regard today's universities as mere extensions of the gymnasium? The gymnasium education embodied in a young person strides through the university gates as something complete and whole, with its own ambitious claims: *it* makes demands, *it* legislates, *it* passes judgment. So do not fool yourselves about the gymnasium graduate: Believing himself to have received the blessings of education, he remains a schoolboy, shaped by his teacher's hands. In academic isolation, having left the gymnasium, he is now beyond the reach of any and every further process of formation and guidance, living from that point forward entirely free and on his own.

"Free! Put this freedom to the test, you connoisseurs of human nature! A freedom built on crumbling foundations, the soft soil of today's gymnasium education, it stands crooked, vulnerable to the breath of the whirling tempest. Take a good look at this free student, herald of independent higher education, and divine him from his instincts, know him by his needs! What will you think of his education when you measure it by the following three yardsticks: his need for philosophy, his instinct for art, and, finally, the standard of Greek and Roman antiquity—the categorical imperative incarnate of all culture?

"We are so beset by serious and difficult problems that, when brought to see them aright, we quickly acquire a lasting philosophical wonder. Only in this fertile soil can a deeper, nobler education grow. Most often, it is a person's own experience that brings him face-to-face with such problems. Especially in tempestuous youth, almost every personal incident shimmers in a double reflection: as an instance of everyday triviality, and at the same time as exemplifying an eternal, mysterious problem that cries out for an answer. At that age, when one sees one's experiences ringed round with metaphysical rainbows, as it were, one's need for a guiding hand is at its most urgent. A young person has suddenly and almost instinctively been convinced of the double meaning of existence, and also lost the firm footing of the beliefs and received opinions he once cherished.

"This great need for guidance is only natural, but clearly the beloved independence for which today's educated young person is groomed could not be more opposed to it. These young men of 'the modern age,' who have hopped into the lap of what is 'self-evident,' are eager to suppress, indeed crush, this need, divert it or deform it, and their favorite method for paralyzing this natural philosophical impulse is through so-called 'historical education.' A philosophical system[9] that only recently enjoyed scandalous, worldwide fame found the formula for this self-destruction of philosophy, and now, in any historical consideration of things, we can see so much reckless naïveté, proving the unreasonable to be 'in accord with reason' and calling the blackest of black 'white,' that one is often tempted to quote Hegel's line as parody: 'Can what is counter to reason be actual?' Alas, today things practically have to be irrational to be 'actual'—that is to say, have real effects—and using actuality in this sense to explain history is seen as the quintessence of 'historical education.' The philosophical instincts of our youth have pupated into this—and the peculiar philosophers of our universities have conspired to reinforce our young scholars' belief in it.

"Historical, in fact philological, considerations have slowly but surely taken the place of any profound exploration of the eternal problems. The question becomes: What did this or that philosopher think or not think? And is this or that text rightly ascribed to him or not? And even: Is this or that variant of a classical text preferable to the other? Students in university philosophy seminars today are encouraged to occupy themselves with such an emasculated philosophy, whereas, for my part, I have long since been accustomed to see such scholarship as a branch of philology, and to judge its practitioners according to whether or not they are good philologists. As a result, of course, *philosophy itself* is banished from the university altogether. With this, our first question about the cultural value of the universities has been answered.

"As for how the university stands in relation to *art,* the truth cannot be admitted without shame—the two stand in no relation whatsoever. Not a trace of artistic thinking, learning, striving, or comparative analysis is to be found there. No one can seriously claim that the university lifts its voice to advance important national artistic projects. An individual professor may happen to feel a personal inclination for art, or an endowed chair may be established for aesthetic-type literary historians, but that is not the point—the fact remains that the university as a whole does not and cannot impose strict artistic discipline on the young people in its charge. It simply lets whatever happens happen, willy-nilly. This is a particularly incisive rebuke to the university's arrogant claim to be the highest educational institution.

"Our 'independent' academics lead their lives without philosophy, without art: Why, then, would they want to have anything to do with the Greeks and Romans, whom no one has to pretend to respect anymore, and who, remote and nearly inaccessible, sit enthroned in majestic strangeness? The universities of today quite logically pay no attention at all to this cultural sense of respect now utterly extinct. They establish their philological professorships solely to rear up future generations of exclusively philological minds, who will in turn be responsible for the philological preparation of gymnasium students—a life cycle that benefits neither the philologists themselves nor the gymnasiums, but which does serve to belie for a third time the university's claim to be what it so proudly poses as: a true educational institution.[10] For take away the Greeks (never mind the Romans), along with philosophy and art, and where is the ladder you can use to ascend to a true education? If you try to climb without these aids, then, I say, all your erudition will weigh heavily on your shoulders instead of giving you wings to bear you aloft.

"If you are honest, and honestly stay with this threefold insight— if you admit that today's students are unprepared for and unsuited to philosophy, lack any artistic instinct, and are mere barbarians with delusions of freedom compared to the Greeks—then you will not flee from these students in disgust, although you might well want to avoid coming too closely in contact with them. For such a student's condition *is not his fault.* The kind of creature you have recognized him to be is merely a silent yet terrible rebuke to those who are truly to blame.

"You have to understand the secret language of these innocents weighed down with guilt: Only then will you be able to understand the inner nature of the independence they so like to show to the outside world. Not one of these nobly equipped young men has avoided the unresting, exhausting, confusing, debilitating crisis of education: He may seem to be the only free man in a world of bureaucrats and slaves, but he pays for this splendid illusion of freedom with constant and ever-growing doubts and torments. He feels that he cannot guide himself, cannot help himself—and then he dives hopelessly into the world of everyday life and daily routine. He is immersed in the *most trivial possible* activity, and his limbs grow weak and weary. Suddenly he pulls himself together—vigorous as ever, he feels the strength that might keep him afloat. Proud and noble resolutions form and grow within him. He is terrified of sinking so soon into the narrow confines of professionalism, and grabs at supports and struts so as not to be swept downstream. But for naught! The supports give way: He has grasped at the wrong thing, tried to hold fast to fragile reeds. In a low and despondent mood, he sees his plans go up in smoke—his condition is sickening and humiliating—he vacillates between exaggerated, bustling activity and melancholy sluggishness: tired, lazy, afraid of work, shrinking back from everything great, full of self-hatred. He analyzes his own abilities and finds, when he peers into himself, only a hollow void or chaotic mess. Then he plummets once more from the heights of imagined self-knowledge into ironic skepticism. He sees his struggles as utterly meaningless and declares himself ready for any task, however low and humble, so long as it is real and useful. Now he seeks consolation in frantic, incessant busyness—anything behind which he can hide from himself. And so his perplexity, his lack of a leader to guide him to true education, drives him from one way of life into another. Doubt, elation, affliction, hope, despair, everything hurls him this way and that, a sign that the stars overhead he could have used to steer his ship have all gone out.

"And that is how this famous independence, this academic freedom, looks when seen through the fate of the best souls, those with the deepest need for education and culture. Compared to these, the cruder and more easygoing natures who enjoy their freedom in the purely barbaric sense count for nothing. With their low pleasures and premature professional narrowness, they fit perfectly into this so-called freedom—who would deny it. Their satisfaction, though, does not outweigh the suffering of even a single young man drawn to culture, in need of a guide, who at last gets discouraged, lets drop the reins, and begins to despise himself. *He* is the guiltless innocent. For who weighed him down with the unbearable burden of standing alone? Who urged him to be independent, at an age when the desire to devote oneself to a great leader, follow enthusiastically in a master's footsteps, is practically one's most urgent and natural need?

"It is troubling to think about what happens when this noble need is so violently crushed. Give a close and penetrating look at the most dangerous friends and advocates of today's despicable pseudo-culture and you will all too often find men who have suffered this degenerate and derailed education, now driven by inner desperation to a furious rage against a culture that no one was willing to show them how to reach. It is not the worst men, not the lowest, whom we later meet as journalists and feuilletonists after they have undergone the metamorphosis of despair; certain well-groomed literary types nowadays might well be characterized as essentially desperate students.[11] How else can we make sense of the once-famous Young Germany movement,[12] whose epigones continue to proliferate today? Here we have a desire for culture that has gone to seed as it were, finally driven to cry out: I am culture, *I am!* In such a movement, the culture that has escaped the gymnasiums and universities now hangs around the gates of these institutions, with a superior air but without, of course, any of these institutions' scholarly erudition. The novelist Karl Gutzkow, for instance, can best be understood as the spitting image of the modern, already literary gymnasium schoolboy.

"It is a serious thing, a man of such degenerate culture, and it is frightening indeed to see that our whole educated reading public bears the mark of this degeneration. When our educated men ceaselessly read journalists, and even cooperate in their work of corrupting the people, we have no choice but to suppose that their erudition is functioning for them much as writing novels functions for others: as a flight from themselves, a desperate self-annihilation, an ascetic strangulation of their own drive for education and culture. The same sigh gushes forth from our degenerate literature and the senselessly bloated book-scribbling of our scholars: *How could we so have lost sight of ourselves?!* But the effort fails: Whole mountains of printed pages are shoveled on but memory refuses to be stifled, and every so often it repeats the refrain: 'Man of degenerate culture! Born to education, and raised in miseducation! Helpless barbarian, slave to the present, lying in the chains of the passing moment, and hungering—always, eternally hungering!'

"Oh these miserable innocents who are held to account! There is something they do not have, and every last one of them must have felt the lack of it: a true educational institution, which could provide them with goals, masters, methods, models, companions, and the invigorating, uplifting breath of the true German spirit streaming up from within it. Instead, these creatures waste away in the wilderness; they degenerate into enemies of the very spirit that is, at bottom, so like their own; they heap guilt upon guilt, more than any generation ever has, sullying what is pure, desecrating what is holy, canonizing what is false and fake. In them you can see what power our universities have to shape culture. Ask yourself, in all seriousness: What is it that you are promoting with these institutions? German erudition, German ingenuity, the honest German drive for knowledge, German hard work capable of any sacrifice—splendid and beautiful things, the envy of other nations, the most splendid and beautiful things in the world, in fact, as long as that other, true German spirit lies outspread over them like a dark thundercloud, aflash with lightning and bursting with the fruitful benediction of the rain. Instead, you live in fear of that spirit, and thus it is a heavy and oppressive fog that has gathered around your universities, and in this miasma your noble young scholars breathe heavily and laboriously, and the best of them perish.

"Earlier this century, a tragically earnest attempt was made to dispel this fog and open a view onto the distant empyrean of the German spirit. The episode is uniquely instructive, since the history of the universities knows of no similar effort, and there is no clearer example of what we now need to do. I am speaking of the old, original *Burschenschaft*.[13]

"These young men brought home from the war the most unexpected, and worthy, trophy of battle: freedom for the fatherland. Crowned with this laurel, they dreamed of something higher still. Our young man who returned to the university found himself gasping in the oppressive, contaminated air that hung over the places of higher education. Eyes wide with horror, he suddenly saw the un-German barbarism artfully hidden beneath academic erudition of all kinds; suddenly he discovered that his own comrades, lacking a leader, had been abandoned to a noxious youthful frenzy. And he was outraged.

"He rose up with the same look of proud indignation that Schiller might have had on his face as he recited *The Robbers* to his companions; Schiller published his play with an image of a lion and the motto *in tyrannos*, but this young man now returning to the university was himself that lion preparing to spring—and every 'tyrant' truly did tremble.[14] Yes, to timid and superficial observers these outraged youths seemed not so different from Schiller's robbers; to anxious listeners, the youths' speeches made Rome and Sparta seem mere nunneries in comparison. The shock and fear these outraged young men inspired was more widespread than anything the 'robbers' ever caused in court circles—although, as Goethe reports, one German prince did apparently remark that if he were God and had foreseen these robbers, he would never have created the world.

"What gave rise to the senseless intensity of this terror? These outraged young men were the bravest, most talented, and purest-hearted men of their generation, distinguished in dress and deportment by a blithely magnanimous spirit and a noble simplicity of morals; magnificent vows bound them together in the service of strict and pious discipline—what was there to be afraid of? It will never be known to what extent those who feared these youths were fooling themselves, or fooling others, or recognizing the truth—but a strong instinct was at work, in this fear and in the disgraceful, senseless persecution that followed. The *Burschenschaft* was instinctively hated, with burning hatred, for two reasons: because its organization represented the first attempt to create a true educational institution; and because this institution's spirit was the manly, serious, somber, hardy, bold German spirit, the spirit of Luther the miner's son, preserved unbroken from the time of the Reformation.

"Now keep in mind the *fate* of the *Burschenschaft* when I ask you: Did the German universities of the time understand that spirit, the way even the German princes in their hatred apparently understood it? Did the university courageously throw her arms around her noblest progeny, shouting: 'To kill them you will have to kill me first!'? I can hear you answer...and you must judge by that answer whether or not the German university is a true educational institution.

"The *Burschenschaft* student of that time sensed how deeply an educational institution needs to take root: all the way down, in the inner renewal and inspiration of the purest moral capacities. And let this be retold always, to his credit. Perhaps he learned on the battlefield what he was hardly likely to learn in today's realm of 'academic freedom': that we need great leaders, and that all education begins with obedience. So, amid the jubilation of victory, he thought of his liberated fatherland and vowed to remain German. German! Now at last he understood Tacitus; now he grasped Kant's categorical imperative; now he was ravished by the songs of Carl Maria von Weber's *Lyre and Sword*.[15] The gates of philosophy, of art, even of antiquity sprang open before him. And in one of the most memorable bloody deeds in our history—the murder of Kotzebue[16]—deep instincts and shortsighted enthusiasm led him to avenge his one and only Schiller, ground down all too soon by the resistance of the obtuse world: Schiller, who could have been his leader, master, and organizer, and whose loss he now lamented with such heartfelt fury.

"Such, true to their forebodings, was these students' undoing: They never found the leader they needed. Gradually they came to doubt each other, and grew dissatisfied and disunited; all too quickly, unhappy missteps revealed the lack of a dauntless genius in their midst. They were leaderless—and it destroyed them.

"For I repeat, my friends! All education begins with the exact opposite of what everyone praises so highly today as 'academic freedom.' It begins in obedience, subordination, discipline, servitude. And just as great leaders need followers, so too must the led have a leader. A certain reciprocal predisposition prevails in the hierarchy of the spirit: yes, a kind of pre-established harmony. The eternal hierarchy that all things naturally gravitate toward is just what the so-called culture now sitting on the throne of the present aims to overturn and destroy. This 'culture' wants to bring leaders down to the level of *its* compulsory servitude, or kill them off altogether; it waylays foreordained followers searching high and low for the one who is to lead them, while its intoxications deaden even their instinct to seek. If, though, wounded and battle-weary, the two sides destined for each other find a way to come together at last, the result is a deep, thrilling bliss that resounds like the strings of an eternal lyre.

"Only with the aid of a metaphor can I convey something of this feeling. Have you ever been to a concert rehearsal and really looked at the strange, shriveled, good-natured subspecies of humanity that typically makes up a German orchestra? What flights of fancy on the part of that capricious goddess, Form! What noses and ears, what clumsy movements and skeletal clattering! Imagine for a moment you were deaf and had never dreamed of the existence of music and melodies, and that you were asked to appreciate an orchestra's movements as a purely physical performance: Untroubled by the idealizing effects of the music, you would never be able to get enough of the sight of this comedy, crude like a medieval woodcut—this innocent caricature of *Homo sapiens.*

"Now imagine your hearing has returned, your ears have opened, and up in front of the orchestra a worthy conductor is performing his assigned task. The comedy of the arrangement is gone; you hear—but no, what our worthy conductor seems to communicate to his fellow musicians is the spirit of boredom. You see nothing but flabby effeminacy, hear nothing but rhythmic inaccuracy, melodic mediocrity, emotional triviality. For you, the orchestra has become a mere crowd, mildly annoying if not downright distasteful.

"Now, however, let your imagination soar, and put a genius—a real genius—in the midst of this mass. You perceive an immediate, incredible transformation. It is as if, by a kind of instantaneous transmigration of the soul, he has entered into all of these half-bestial bodies so that they all gaze out with a single daemonic eye. Look and listen now—you will never see or hear your fill! When you regard the orchestra now, in its sublime tempests or heartfelt laments—when you sense the agile tension of every muscle and the rhythmic necessity of their every movement—then you too will feel what constitutes a pre-established harmony between leader and led, and how, in the hierarchy of spirits, everything pushes toward this kind of organization. From this simile of mine, you can guess what I understand a true educational institution to be, and why I cannot in any way see the university as such a place."

NIETZSCHE'S INTRODUCTION AND PREFACE

EDITORS' NOTE

We do not know what prompted Nietzsche to abandon his lectures on education, but in December 1872, he reported to a friend that he had struggled with how to conclude them, confessing that he had failed in his attempts to flesh out a final lecture.

Nietzsche wrote the introduction that follows sometime in 1872 after he delivered the lectures. And, when he still thought he might publish the lectures, he wrote a preface for the book version, which he sent along with four other prefaces to Cosima Wagner in December, under the title "Five Prefaces to Five Unwritten Books." The collection was meant to be a birthday present.

Introduction

THE TITLE I have given my lectures—"On the Future of Our Educational Institutions"—is meant to be as focused, clear, and vivid as possible: the duty of any title. But it is, I now realize, excessively focused, and thus too short, and hence unclear as well. I must therefore begin by explaining to my honored listeners, and excusing if need be, the title and with it the task of these lectures.

When I promised to speak about the future of our educational institutions, I did not have in mind Basel's institutions in particular. No matter how often they seem perfectly suited to illustrate my general claims, I am not the one using them to do so, and I do not want to be held responsible if my argument is applied in that way. If for no other reason than that I consider myself a stranger here, much too inexperienced, too little rooted in local circumstances, to judge the specific educational arrangements here properly, much less sketch out their future with any confidence. Then again, I am certainly well aware that I am giving these lectures in a city-republic that promotes the culture and education of its citizens with uncommon generosity, and on a scale that puts larger states to shame. Surely I am not wrong in assuming that here, where one *does* so much more for culture and education, one must *think* about them more as well. Such is my hope, and indeed a prerequisite of these lectures: that I am in an intellectual exchange with listeners who have not only thought about questions of education and culture but are ready to support with their actions the principles they have recognized as right. Given the scope of my task and the little time I have, I can make myself understood only to listeners such as these: who guess at once what can only be hinted at, who fill in what must be left hidden, in short, who need only be reminded, not taught.

You must therefore not see me as giving unsolicited advice about Basel's schools and educational policies. I am even less inclined to predict the future of education and various educational methods across the universe of different national cultures. My vision fails before the monstrous expanse of this horizon, just as it blurs whenever something is too close. What I mean, then, when I say "our" educational institutions is neither Basel's in particular nor the countless others in the far-flung nations of the present. I mean the *German institutions of higher learning* that we have been pleased to adopt here in Switzerland as well. It is the future of these institutions that concerns us: the future of the German *Volksschule*, *Realschule*, gymnasium, and university.[1]

Let us set aside any comparison or value judgment, and take special care not to succumb to the flattering delusion that our situation is exemplary and unsurpassed compared to everywhere else. The fact is that these schools are ours: not part of our culture by chance, not draped over us like a gown. As living monuments of important cultural movements, like "our grandfathers' old curiosities,"[2] they link us to our nation's past. In essence, they are such a sacred and venerable legacy that when I speak of their future, I am merely trying as best I can to approximate the ideal spirit out of which they were born. I am firmly convinced that the many changes to these institutions we have permitted ourselves to make, in an effort to ensure they are "up to date," are largely deviations and lapses from the original lofty impulse with which they were founded. In this light, what I dare to hope for from the future is a revitalization, renewal, and purification of the German spirit, so all-encompassing that these institutions will be largely reborn from that spirit as well. After such a rebirth, they will be old and new at once, while today they can at best merely claim to be "modern" and "up to date."

Only with this hope in mind do I speak of the future of our educational institutions: This is the second point I want to make up front in my own defense. Nothing is more presumptuous than to want to be a prophet, and so to announce that one has no intention of being a prophet sounds simply ridiculous. No one should try to strike an oracular note about our culture's future, and the related future of our educational means and methods, if he cannot prove that this culture of the future is to some extent already present and need only assert itself much more strongly to have the requisite influence on schools and other pedagogical institutions. Permit me merely to predict the future out of the entrails of the present, like a Roman haruspice, which in this case involves neither more nor less than predicting the eventual victory of an educational tendency that already exists, even if at the moment it is neither popular, nor respected, nor widely prevalent. But it will triumph, I say with supreme confidence, because it has the greatest and mightiest ally of all: *Nature*. Which is not to deny, of course, that many of the premises of our modern educational methods are in fact unnatural, nor that the catastrophic failings of today have everything to do with these unnatural methods.

We do not envy the people who feel completely at home in the present and consider contemporary conditions "self-evident"—neither for this belief of theirs nor for this scandalously intellectual term "self-evident," so in vogue nowadays. People who have come to the opposite conclusion, and have already fallen into despair—they, too, need fight no more. Let them surrender to isolation and solitude. However, somewhere between these "self-evident" types and the loners stand the *fighters*: those full of hope, whose noblest and most exalted example we see in our great Schiller, as depicted for us in Goethe's epilogue to "The Song of the Bell":[3]

> Brighter glowed his cheek, and still more bright,
> With that unfading ever-youthful glow,
> The courage that prevails in hard-fought fight
> Over the resistance of the obtuse world,
> Now pressing on so fast, now patient, slow,
> So that the good might prosper, grow more free,
> And give the day its true nobility.

Honored listeners, take what I have said thus far as a foreword, intended merely to explain the title of these lectures and guard it against possible misunderstanding and unjustified criticism. Now, to pass without further delay from title to substance, let me here, at the entryway to my reflections, describe the general perspective from which I mean to judge our educational institutions. A clearly formulated thesis here at the threshold, like a coat of arms, should serve to remind all who approach whose house and estate they are about to set foot in—unless, after scrutinizing this coat of arms, they prefer instead to turn their back on the house and estate thus labeled.

My thesis is as follows:

Our educational institutions, originally built upon entirely different foundations, are presently dominated by two tendencies, apparently opposed but equally ruinous in effect and ultimately converging in their end results. One is the drive to *expand education* as much as possible; the other is the drive to *narrow and weaken it*. The first pushes to extend education and culture to an ever-wider circle; the second expects education to give up its highest claim to autonomy and submit to serve another form of life, the state. Given these disastrous tendencies toward overinflation and weakening, one might well succumb to hopeless despair—were it not possible to help two opposing forces to eventual victory. These opposing tendencies, thoroughly German and full of promise for the future, are the drive to *narrow and concentrate* education, counteracting its ever-increasing expansion, and the drive to make education *strong and self-sufficient*, counteracting its diminishment. What justifies our faith in the possibility of victory is the knowledge that the first two tendencies, to inflation and weakening, run counter to Nature's eternally invariable intentions, just as concentrating education in the few is a necessary law of that same Nature—indeed a *truth*, while the other two tendencies can only create a culture of lies.

Preface

TO BE READ BEFORE THE LECTURES, ALTHOUGH IT
DOES NOT REFER TO THEM

THE READER I hope for must have three qualities: He must read
calmly, without haste; he mustn't always let himself and his "culture" intrude into his reading; and finally, he must not expect a concrete result, some tables and charts at the end. I have no charts and
no revised gymnasium or *Realschule* timetables to offer. Truth be
told, I can only marvel at the towering energy of those who survey
the entire path from the depths of the empirical up to the heights of
real cultural problems, and then come back down it to traverse the
barren lowlands of regulations at their most arid, charts at their
most meticulous. I myself am satisfied when, gasping for breath, I
have clambered up a relatively high mountain and can enjoy a clear
view. The present book will never satisfy the chart lovers.

I can imagine a time when serious people, working together in
the service of a renewed and purified cultural education, will once
again legislate over the everyday instruction meant to lead to that
new education. They will probably draw up tables and charts then,
too. But how far in the future that era lies! How much has to happen
before then! Between now and that time to come may lie the destruction of the gymnasium, maybe even the destruction of the university, or at least a restructuring of these educational institutions so
complete that their old charts and tables will look like Bronze Age
relics.

This book is meant for calm readers, those who have not yet been
caught up in the dizzying haste of our hurtling era and do not yet feel
an idolatrous pleasure in being crushed under its wheels—in other
words, it is a book for the few. These few cannot bring themselves to

judge a thing on the basis of how much time it saves or wastes: They "still have time." They still allow themselves to choose and gather the best hours and most productive and powerful moments of the day, to spend them in reflection on our culture's future, without self-reproach. They even think they have spent such days well, in a truly useful and worthy manner, namely in *meditatio generis futuri*.[1] Someone like this has not yet unlearned how to think. As he reads, he still understands the secret of reading between the lines; he is even inefficient enough to *think* about what he has read, sometimes long after he has put down his book! And not to write a review, or another book, but just like that, just to think! It's criminal, to be so wasteful. He is calm and unworried enough to set out with the author on a long road whose endpoint only a much later generation will see. When the greatly agitated reader, in contrast, springs into action, wants to pluck fruit hard-won over decades and centuries, and pluck them *now*, then we must fear he has failed to understand the author.

Finally, the third and most important requirement is this: Under no circumstances may the reader constantly take himself and his cultural attainments to be the measure and criterion of all things, as modern man is so wont to do. Let him be educated enough to think little of his own education, think scornfully even; then he can confidently follow the lead of an author who ventures to address him only from a place of ignorance, a perspective of knowing that he does not know. This author claims for himself nothing more than a burning sense of what is specific to our contemporary German barbarism— what distinguishes us nineteenth-century barbarians so remarkably from the barbarians of earlier times.

He searches, this book in his hand, for others who are driven from pillar to post by similar feelings. Show yourselves, you singular individuals—I still believe you exist! You selfless ones, suffering inwardly the sorrows and depravities of the German spirit; you contemplative ones, whose eyes do not just glance quickly at the surface of things but find a way into their essential core; you great-hearted ones, whom Aristotle praised for going through life hesitant and

idle except where a great honor calls you and a great work needs you!
It is to you I appeal! This time, do not crawl into your caves of isolation and mistrust! At least be readers of this book, so that later,
through your actions, you can consign it to destruction and obliv-
ion. Think of it as your herald; once you appear on the battlefield in
person, in armor of your own, who then will care to look back at the
herald who summoned you?

NOTES

1   This is not to suggest that the position would have been thought of as a particularly desirable one. Professorships in Germany were more prestigious and better paid, and the University of Basel made a practice of hiring talented young men from the German system knowing that they would likely return to it after a few years, as Nietzsche's predecessor had. Still, the city was beautiful, with a patrician attachment to classical learning that was a good match for Nietzsche culturally. For a twenty-four-year-old student (who hadn't even been looking for work), to land the job was a quite a coup. In what was an accepted practice, the University of Leipzig awarded him a doctorate on the basis of the articles he had published in a scholarly journal. To hold a comparable position at a German institution would have required a second major project: the *Habilitationsschrift*.

2   Friedrich Nietzsche, *Nietzsches Briefwechsel: Kritische Gesamtausgabe*, edited by Giorgio Colli and Mazzino Montinari (Berlin: Walter de Gruyter, 1975–2004), 1.2, 248.

3   Rüdiger Safranski, *Nietzsche: A Philosophical Biography*, translated by Shelley Frisch (New York: W.W. Norton and Company, 2002), 53.

4   Nietzsche, *Nietzsches Briefwechsel*, 2.1, 155.

5   The *Realschule* was the more practical, vocational parallel track to the gymnasium. Up until the late nineteenth century, the only way to university study was the gymnasium, a nine-year course of study that included Greek, Latin, religion, physics, history, literature, mathematics, and natural history.

6   Of course, the term anti-academic isn't meant to suggest that Nietzsche
     was dismissive of all academics and all academic knowledge. He continued
     to profess his admiration for Ritschl, and in developing his ideas about
     such things as history and human perception, Nietzsche drew on an array
     of academic works in philosophy, philology, and the sciences. Our point
     is simply that he became generally suspicious of academic knowledge. No
     longer was the main problem that it was so often lifeless and boring;
     generally speaking, academic knowledge played a key part in creating
     and perpetuating the malaise of modernity. Eventually, Nietzsche would
     also come to see the academic value of objectivity, the goals of attaining
     a disinterested, disembodied perspective and of identifying truths un-
     tainted by the contingencies of their historical contexts, as a form of
     nihilism—at once the destroyer of Christianity and the heir to Christian
     nihilism. Readers interested in the evolution of Nietzsche's critique of aca-
     demic knowledge might, for example, consider places where his *Untimely
     Meditations* (1876), and especially the essay "On the Advantage and Dis-
     advantage of History for Life," build upon ideas he began to develop in
     the Basel lectures, which offer a critique of the optimistic "historical cul-
     ture" that he debunks in greater detail in the "On the Advantage" essay.

7   In fairness, higher education was less expensive in Germany than in, say,
     England. In the 1870s Germany outpaced both France and England
     with regard to the percentage of the population that attained a univer-
     sity degree, thanks in part to policies meant to help students from mod-
     est backgrounds, such as the deferral of student fees (*Stundung*). But the
     German educational system clearly failed to live up to the ideals of in-
     clusiveness established by its nineteenth-century architects, who
     strongly believed that everyone would benefit from classical study and
     merit, much more than means, should determine who has access to elite
     education. And so those nineteenth-century figures who liked to boast
     about the system's meritocratic nature—e.g., the historian of education
     Friedrich Paulsen—were drastically overstating the case.

8   Due in part to hysteria about the subversive potential of a large group of
     unemployed people with university training, the government rolled
     back some of its more inclusive policies at the school conference of 1890.
     With the economy fuming along, government changed course a decade
     later. By the beginning of the First World War, the number of university
     students in Germany had swelled to 60,000. The gymnasium prolifer-

ated rapidly but not quite as explosively. In 1859, there were 133 schools and 38,681 students in the German territories; by 1871 these numbers had grown to 205 and 59,031; and in 1914 they stood at 346 and 101,745. Population growth alone cannot account for this increase: During the *Kaiserreich*, the population of Germany expanded from 40,089,000 to 64,926,000.

9   Suzanne L. Marchand, *Down from Olympus: Archaeology and Philhellenism in Germany, 1750–1970* (Princeton, NJ: Princeton University Press, 1996), 31.

10   Lorraine Daston, "The Academies and the Unity of Knowledge: Disciplining the Disciplines," *Differences* 10, 2 (Summer 1998): 67–86. On the emergence of modern disciplines and the culture of specialization, which had more causes than can be listed here, see Chad Wellmon, *Organizing Enlightenment: Information Overload and the Invention of the Modern Research University* (Baltimore, MD: Johns Hopkins University Press, 2015).

11   Johann Voss quoted in Anthony Grafton, "Polyhistor to Philolog: Notes on the Transformation of German Classical Scholarship, 1780–1850," *History of Universities* 3 (1983), 173.

12   See Hermann von Helmholtz, "Über das Verhältnis der Naturwissenschaften zur Gesammtheit der Wissenschaft," in *Vorträge und Reden*, vol. 1 (Braunschweig: Vieweg und Sohn, 1903), 158–85.

13   Nietzsche had a complex and fascinating relationship to the natural sciences. He was critical of the culture of scientific objectivity, among other things, but he also thought that scientific experiments having to do with human perception might demonstrate the impossibility of objective thought. See Christian J. Emden, *Nietzsche's Naturalism: Philosophy and the Life Sciences in the Nineteenth Century* (Cambridge: Cambridge University Press, 2014).

14   Ibid., 38.

15   Early on, Nietzsche saw Basel as a peaceful patrician refuge that provided a good vantage point from which to criticize Germany. When *The Birth of Tragedy* was greeted with controversy, he wrote that he was distressed "because I am truly dedicated, as well as grateful, to our little University, and the last thing I would want is to cause it harm." Also worth noting here is that with unification in 1871, the political coloration

of German academia changed dramatically, becoming far more patriotic and intent on mobilizing scholarship in support of the Prussian state, while of course (mostly) maintaining the ideal of scholarship for its own sake; so not only was Nietzsche criticizing Germany, he was doing so at a time when the current at German universities had begun to flow strongly the other way. Later, his attitude toward Basel would become more complex—and ambivalent. Cited in Gossman, *Basel in the Age of Burckhardt*, 430.

16 The hall in which the lectures were delivered, which seated more than three hundred, was consistently filled.

17 Nietzsche's lectures in 1872 were not, however, a farewell to academia, an ur-example of what is now known as "quit lit." Nietzsche held on to his professorship for another seven years, and during that time took his teaching responsibilities seriously, even formally proposing improvements to the Greek curriculum at the gymnasium where he taught. With *On the Future of Our Educational Institutions*, he was joining a reform-minded conversation about German higher education, rather than opting out. Several of Nietzsche's proposals were in fact accepted, such as the textbook he recommended for all forms (Ernst Koch's *Griechische Schulgrammatik*, 1869) and his suggestion that Greek be mandatory for all students. By all accounts a popular and effective teacher, he looked back with pride on his experience at the gymnasium in Basel, writing in *Ecce Homo* that he "never once had occasion to mete out a punishment; even the laziest students were industrious when they were with me." Friedrich Nietzsche, *Ecce homo*, in *Nietzsche Werke*, 1:3, 267.

18 Another factor here may have been the difficulty of Nietzsche's position with the field of philology after the publication of *The Birth of Tragedy* in 1872. This instantly made him into something of a pariah; his relationship with Ritschl was compromised and enrollment in his courses plummeted. Both bothered Nietzsche, who continued to correspond with Ritschl about producing more traditional philological work. Nietzsche didn't ultimately pursue the sorts of projects that might have won Ritschl's approval. But he wasn't quite ready to burn all his bridges to the philological establishment. "We Philologists," which was to expand the criticisms of philology in *On the Future of Our Educational Institutions* (and does so in notational form), and which was to be the fourth Untimely Meditation, remained unpublished, too.

19   See Mark Edmundson, *Why Teach? In Defense of a Real Education* (New York: Bloomsbury USA, 2013); William Deresiewicz, *Excellent Sheep: The Miseducation of the American Elite and the Way to a Meaningful Life* (New York: The Free Press, 2014); and Andrew Delbanco, *College: What It Was, What It Is, and What It Should Be* (Princeton, NJ: Princeton University Press, 2011).

20   Delbanco, *College*, 159, 140.

21   David Armitage et al, "The Teaching of the Arts and Humanities at Harvard College: Mapping the Future," available at artsandhumanities.fas.harvard.edu/files/humanities/files/mapping_the_future_31_may_2013.pdf.

22   Delbanco, *College*, 179.

23   This is an odd choice of evidence; after all, the challenge of working with career-oriented students in required humanities classes is quite different from and in some ways more difficult than working with students for whom a humanities seminar is a rare opportunity and something new, and who have come to the seminar voluntarily.

24   In fairness, neither Edmundson nor Deresiewicz nor Delbanco posits a golden age of academia that the present one has supplanted. Deresiewicz, for example, stresses the historical injustices of American higher education in his compact survey of it. But they all believe that things have changed fundamentally—for the worse. The following line by Deresiewicz is typical: "college used to be understood as a time to experiment with different selves, of whatever type. Now students all seem to be converging on the same self, the successful, upper-middle-class professional they've already decided they want to become." See Deresiewicz, *Excellent Sheep*, 24.

LECTURE I

1   Between January 16 and March 23, 1872, Nietzsche delivered "On the Future of Our Educational Institutions" as a series of public lectures in Basel's city museum. He had recently turned twenty-seven, and his youth was unusual for a professor but certainly not unheard-of. Still, several years earlier when Nietzsche received the offer to come to Basel, his inexperience was such that Friedrich Ritschl, his illustrious adviser,

had to convince the hiring committee that his young student was ready for the job. In his recommendation, Ritschl claimed to be willing to "stake [his] whole academic reputation" on Nietzsche's future success.

2 In ancient Rome, haruspices were a kind of priest who practiced a form of divination based on the inspection of entrails. They specialized in interpreting events that portended possible political disaster. After the haruspices performed their ritual, the Senate would convene to discuss possible courses of action; Cicero describes this in, for example, *De haruspicum responsis*.

3 Basel's city museum is in a stately neoclassical building on Augustinergasse. Funded solely by membership subscriptions, it was a center of activity for the cultured elite, housing not only municipal collections but also meeting rooms for learned societies and auditoriums for public talks. In short, the museum was built for and remained dedicated to civic education and culture: It was a space for public humanities. Nietzsche's lectures were announced on the same program as Jacob Burckhardt's "On Happiness and Unhappiness in World History," something that probably pleased Nietzsche, given his admiration for Burckhardt (the author of *The Civilization of the Renaissance in Italy*, 1860).

Attendance at Nietzsche's lectures was good and the response to them quite positive. Nietzsche boasted about the "sensation" they unleashed. On the other hand, he also groused about a "stupid review" in a local newspaper that "misunderstood everything I was trying to say."

4 For centuries, Basel had enjoyed a city-state status that contributed to its political autonomy and cultural particularity. In the last third of the nineteenth century, it was, as Lionel Gossman has put it, a "sanctuary" for scholars in the neo-humanist mold. When he arrived in Basel in 1869, Nietzsche encountered a culture steeped in classical humanism and proud of its reverence for antiquity.

In particular, Basel was home to patrician scholars such as Burckhardt and Johann Jakob Bachofen, a critic of contemporary philology and a theorist of myth and matriarchy. Nietzsche admired—and courted—both men, who had their doubts about him. The Basel mandarins were also concerned about the relationship between the state and culture, which partly explains their receptiveness to Nietzsche's lectures.

5 Nietzsche was not above trying to win over his listeners through flattery, which should be kept in mind while reading the dialogue that makes up most of these lectures. Sometimes Nietzsche has his characters utter statements that would have appealed to the intellectual sensibilities of his audience but which surely struck him as dubiously metaphysical, such as the claim that great works should "purely reflect the eternal, unchanging nature of things."

6 Nietzsche spent the 1864–1865 academic year at the University of Bonn. He enrolled as a student of theology but switched to philology, a particular strength of the university at the time. At Bonn, Nietzsche belonged briefly to the Franconia fraternity; the members' traditional penchant for drinking evidently repelled him. For their part, his fraternity brothers tended to regard him as "crazy" (or really, as crazily ascetic) because he spent his free time studying and playing music. Soon after relocating to the University of Leipzig, Nietzsche took his abstemiousness to a new level, swearing off alcohol and tobacco altogether.

7 The gymnasium was the secondary school that prepared students for university. Its nine-year course of study included Greek, Latin, religion, physics, history, literature, mathematics, and natural history; grades were also issued for conduct. Study at the gymnasium culminated with the Abitur—a comprehensive examination that determined university entrance and placement.

   During the seventeenth and eighteenth centuries, the gymnasium was centered on religion. The school day featured religious service, prayer, and the singing of hymns. Greek and Hebrew were learned for the purpose of reading the Bible. But Latin and the study of Latin grammar and literature was really the core of the curriculum. The "Latin school," as this model was called, was in effect a preparatory program for theologians and something to be endured by students with other inclinations. This began to change in the era of Enlightenment. But it was really as a result of the Prussian school reforms of the early nineteenth century that the gymnasium became the institution most closely associated with the classical curriculum and the pedagogical ideal of *Humanitätsbildung*—"the cultivation of humanity"—in individual students.

8 Along with two school friends, Gustav Krug and Wilhelm Pinder, Nietzsche formed such a club. The founding ceremony took place in the shadow of Schönburg, a medieval fortress near Nietzsche's hometown,

in July 1860. The three teenagers called their association Germania; pledged to submit poems, stories, and essays for discussion and constructive critique; and held quarterly meetings for about four years. Neither Krug nor Pinder went with Nietzsche to Bonn, but another gymnasium friend did: Paul Deussen, who belonged to the same fraternity as Nietzsche and shared many of his cultural interests. Thus it's likely that Deussen, too, served as a basis for the friend character in these lectures.

9   Rolandseck is a mountain in the Rhine valley named for the medieval ruin (now restored) that sits atop it: Roland's Arch. Thus, like Nietzsche's nonfictional Germania, the association described in the lectures came into existence in surroundings suggestive of different times.

10   In contrast to American colleges, German universities had no dormitories and provided almost no institutional support for students beyond academics. A host of student associations, from fraternities to more intellectually oriented student clubs and associations, filled this void. At Leipzig, Nietzsche joined the new Philological Club.

11   Fraternities in Germany were famous for dueling; heavy drinking; proudly displaying their color scheme on caps, sashes, and banners; and discouraging studiousness. One nineteenth-century historian went so far as to argue that, in some fraternities, indolence was elevated to the status of a "principle," which was "enforced against obstreperous members with all means within the power of the society." But not all German fraternities did these things; the situation was, in fact, rather complex.

The earliest fraternities, which date to the latter part of the eighteenth century, were frankly elitist. They celebrated aristocratic lineage, as well as regional ties. Dissolute behavior was generally a point of pride for these organizations, which were known as the corps. The beginning of the next century saw the formation of counterinstitutions: the *Burschenschaften*. Founded in the wake of the wars (1803–1815) against Napoleon, the *Burschenschaft* movement, which Nietzsche will praise later in these lectures, strove to imbue student life with political and ethical purpose by making it a central part of the campaign for German national unity. Such loftier purposes demanded a spirit of inclusiveness, high moral fiber, and a willingness to sacrifice. The cause of unity was politically subversive and viewed as a threat to the order established by the Concert of Vienna. Indeed, Metternich cracked down on the *Bur-*

schenschaften in 1819. But it was impossible to suppress them completely, and by Nietzsche's day many fraternities, including the one he belonged to in Bonn, identified with aspects of both the corps tradition and the *Burschenschaft* movement.

12   In the late nineteenth century, dueling was an important activity for most German fraternities, though it had become quite controversial. Some duels were potentially lethal encounters, set up because of a slight against the honor of a fraternity member. Most were done for sport—extreme fencing, really. Fraternities generally required their pledges to participate in such duels. In these events, known as the *Mensur*, thick pads were worn on the body, but the head was uncovered, so that the participants could get the facial scars which they wanted to display as a sign of their courage and virility. Nietzsche's duel at Bonn, in 1865, was of the *Mensur* kind, and according to an eyewitness, it went like this: "The two adversaries bumbled around directing blows at the other's padded arms for the course of eleven minutes. Nietzsche got a superficial cut a little less than an inch long on his nose."

13   The German word for education, here and in the title of the lectures, is *Bildung*, which comes from the verb *bilden* (to form). It has multiple meanings—education, enlightenment, culture, inner development, sculpting or shaping—none of which quite captures its significance. *Bildung* is not simply education but the process, achieved through education, of forming the most desirable self; it is also the ideal endpoint of that process: attaining or undergoing *Bildung* means acquiring and entering true culture. At the end of the eighteenth century, *Bildung* became a key ideal, and many German thinkers weighed in with an attempt to define what that process should be like and where it should lead.

    The present translation uses both "culture" and "education" for *Bildung,* sometimes "culture and education," and uses these terms for other German words as well, such as *Erziehung* (bringing up a young person, sometimes equated with education and sometimes distinguished from it) and *Kultur* ("culture" in a less grand sense, translated where required by context as "pseudo-culture"). Sometimes *Bildung* is "true culture" or "true education," opposed to the wrongheaded *Bildung* that Nietzsche despised. The goal is not a one-to-one correspondence between English and German terms but clarity in each passage. Still, readers should keep in mind that culture ("in the true sense") is the culmination of an education, and education ("in the true sense") transmits and creates culture.

14 Members of Pythagorean communities were *homakoo* (those who come to listen) and the place they gathered was *homokoeion* (a place for hearing together); the teachings could not be shared with those outside the community. Initiates took a vow committing themselves to five years of silence, when they would listen only to Pythagoras. Nietzsche read Pythagoras and considered him an early religious reformer concerned with "sacred customs" that could lead to salvation. Nietzsche also criticized what he took to be the self-denying practices of Pythagorean communities.

15 The phrase alludes to one of Germany's oldest and most important societies: *Die fruchtbringende Gesellschaft*. Founded in 1617 in Weimar in the spirit of the Accademia della Crusca, the Fruitbearing Society was established to promote the use of the German language among scholars and poets, who in the seventeenth century tended to write in Latin or French.

16 In Prussia, all aspiring administrative professionals had the same three-year university course of study, as did would-be judges and attorneys. Afterward they would take an oral and written examination and submit a thesis written over six weeks. Then they had to go through an unpaid training period that was followed by a second exam. After a further period of unpaid training, they were eligible, at last, to sit for the Great State Examination, which was conducted under the authority of the Examining Commission for Higher Administrative Offices in Berlin. This final exam had oral and written components, and covered constitutional and administrative law, political economy, and finance.

17 Despite Nietzsche's call later in these lectures for greater rigor in secondary education, he didn't breeze through the gymnasiums he attended. As a student of the Cathedral Gymnasium in his adopted hometown of Naumburg, he had a D average in his third semester, his best marks being for conduct. And the myth that he received a scholarship to the elite gymnasium Schulpforta on the basis of his intellectual precocity is just that: a myth. Nietzsche qualified for a scholarship under a program to assist orphans and children whose fathers had died, as

Carl Ludwig Nietzsche had. While at Schulpforta, Nietzsche excelled in Greek, but his performance in mathematics was so bad that it almost kept him from graduating.

18   In 1868, Nietzsche penned detailed notes for a planned dissertation entitled "Teleology Since Kant," which often refer to the second half of Immanuel Kant's *The Critique of Judgment* (1790). But it remains unclear how much Kant he actually read. Scholars disagree. Although Nietzsche never wagered a thorough commentary on any of Kant's works, he did voice the occasional critical remark. He was clearly concerned about the dualism that he, like so many before and after him, saw lurking in the Kantian critical system. In *Twilight of the Idols* (1882), for example, he writes that "any distinction between a 'true' and an 'apparent' world" is "a symptom of the devaluing of life."

19   In the United States, public universities have long had to answer the question: How do they benefit society? In nineteenth-century Germany, the question was: What do they do for the state? The University of Göttingen, in some ways the first research university, was established in 1737 primarily as a mercantilist enterprise, whose purpose was to serve the state's financial interests. At the beginning of the nineteenth century, Wilhelm von Humboldt's plans for reform won a measure of autonomy for Prussia's new universities, but they did so by convincing the state that a culture of research autonomy would be of greater use to it than one tied more directly to practical ends. This was by nature a tenuous formula, and in the decades to come it would be tested, even as German scholars and scientists continued to profess their loyalty to the ideal of pursuing knowledge for the sake of knowledge alone.

20   It was Karl Marx who coined the term that Nietzsche is drawing on here: *Nationalökonomie*. Marx did so to describe the classical liberal economic thinking of Adam Smith, David Ricardo, and J. S. Mill. The late nineteenth-century German version of national economy tended to be more technocratic than its classical forebears, but it did follow Mill, whom Nietzsche particularly disliked for his emphasis on making the individual useful to the state. Here usefulness was understood in terms of economic productivity. In addition, Nietzsche had had a bad experience with national-economic thinking at the University of Bonn; the lectures of the national-economist Wilhelm Roscher, which he found depressingly "narrow," disappointed him in the extreme. It's worth noting

that "national economist" was and would remain a fairly broad cate-gory—it was the term the sociologist Max Weber would use to describe himself in *Science as a Vocation* (1919).

21 Kant described the university as a factory for the production of special-ized knowledge. "It was not a bad idea," he wrote in *The Conflict of the Faculties* (1798), "to treat the entire content of learning (actually the minds devoted to it) in a factory-like manner through a division of la-bor." As a division of *labor*, this process focused on organizing the peo-ple who produced knowledge. There would be "as many public teachers, professors, trustees" as there were "categories of science." Taken together, he concluded, these teachers would constitute a kind of "learned com-munity called a university." Between the time Kant wrote admiringly of an intellectual division of labor and the time of Nietzsche's lectures, the German research university had expanded the logic of academic special-ization to unparalleled levels.

22 Academic specialization in German universities was justified, "cloaked" as Nietzsche puts it, by an idealist vision of scholarship that extended back to Humboldt, Friedrich Schleiermacher, and their contempo-raries. Given the surfeit of information and the finitude of human life and abilities, no scholar could bring forth a comprehensive account of all knowledge, not even in his own field. But what he could do was spe-cialize and reduce his purview to a form of labor and inquiry that was more manageable. And by doing so as part of a transhistorical commu-nity of fellow scholars, he contributed to the progressive and unending project of human knowledge. However specialized and rarified his par-ticular academic work might be, he was participating in something much greater than himself. Here is this vision in Schleiermacher's word-ing, from "Occasional Thoughts on German Universities" (1808): "All efforts at true scholarship exert a centrifugal pull on the others and tend to flow together into one. And there can hardly be any area of human activity that rivals scholarship in forming such wide community and in having been, from its very beginnings, such a continuously running tra-dition." But keeping this vision alive would prove more difficult than Schleiermacher suggested. As the culture of specialization advanced, and scholars in different fields had less to say to each other, it became harder to imagine how each individual scholar was playing a role in a collective endeavor that extended beyond his own discipline.

23 The word Nietzsche uses here is *Wissenschaft*, "body of knowledge." Generally speaking, *Wissenschaft* means science but not necessarily a natural science like physics or biology: it means systematic knowledge and scholarship of all kinds, even history or literary criticism. Like *Bildung*, *Wissenschaft* is both a practice and a product: what scholars and scientists do, and what they create. The present translation uses various terms alone or in combination, such as "science," "scholarship," "field," and "academic knowledge."

LECTURE II

1 Newspaper German—*Zeitungsdeutsch*—was a popular term of opprobrium in the last third of the nineteenth century. It was meant to evoke the degraded language of journalism. One critic made the word into a title, basing his querulous work *Newspaper German* (1883) on examples of bad German clipped from newspapers. The press, he claimed, was "corrupting our German"; it had caused the Germans' linguistic "sickness," which had reached epidemic proportions. "Today everyone writes and speaks however he wants, and has no regard at all for the rules." The critic went on to describe the proliferation of journalistic neologisms, which had "sprung up like mushrooms"; the abuse of idioms; the failure to deploy German declination and conjunctions properly; the poor use of adjectives. Or as the Austrian critic Karl Kraus, who spent a lot of ink underlining the grammatical mistakes of journalists, would put it a few decades later, "the newspaper now speaks like the world, because the world speaks like the newspaper."

2 Nietzsche is referring to the *Gelehrtenschule* of the eighteenth century—the "scholars' school" or "school of erudition." This was a gymnasium in which the focus was on the study of theology and Latin rather than on some kind of inner humanistic development on the part of the students. But at least students learned something there—this is what Nietzsche is saying. Interested readers can find a memorable description of the *Gelehrtenschule* in the early parts of Karl Philipp Moritz's autobiographical novel *Anton Reiser* (1785–1790).

3 Nietzsche would turn to the question of history in the second of his *Untimely Meditations*, "On the Advantages and Disadvantages of History for Life" (1874). "Certainly," he wrote, "we need history, but we need it differently than the spoiled idler in the garden of knowledge

needs it." We need history only in its life-enhancing capacity: "This means that we need history for life and for deeds, not for a comfortable turning away from life....We should serve history only insofar as it serves life." From there Nietzsche proceeded to pick up directly on the critique of philology he had begun developing in these lectures, adding that the "sole purpose" of "classical philology" should be to use ancient history "to work against the present moment" and "hopefully for future ones." Yet philologists do just the opposite, using antiquity as material for carrying out modern research designs that are completely foreign to the spirit of their material.

4   One wouldn't want to read Nietzsche's lectures to get a precise sense of how things stood with German gymnasiums, but in fairness to him, the definitive history of the gymnasium German essay in the late nineteenth century, Otto Ludwig's *The School Essay* (1988), broadly supports Nietzsche's claim here. The German essay had once been an exercise in classical rhetoric. With the rise of neo-humanism in the Enlightenment era, pedagogical practices began to change, but slowly and fitfully. Thus in Nietzsche's day, the German essay remained a topic of debate, with progressive reformers asking such questions as: "How can a youth who has even a somewhat lively mind work with pleasure and passion when he is bound to pre-established forms?" As one commentator put it, the pedagogical goals changed in such a way that less emphasis was put on "a display of rhetorical expertise" and more on the "subjective needs of the writing subject."

5   The "churning out of books"—*Buchmacherei*—was another well-established term of censure, typically invoked to condemn the reduction of publishing to a mere commercial enterprise that let the whims of the market determine the activities of the intellect. Kant, for example, used it in this way, about Friedrich Nicolai, a famous Berlin publisher who put out books in "a factory-like manner."

6   This is a somewhat tricky distinction, since elsewhere Nietzsche mocks the "man of culture." In the essay "Schopenhauer as Educator" (1874), we find this claim: "The man of culture has devolved into the greatest enemy of culture." But there Nietzsche was referring to the person who counted in Wilhelmine Germany as a man of culture—that is, to the man of culture as defined by the standards of the day, which he saw determined by the prevailing "pseudo-culture." That man of culture was,

for Nietzsche, an enemy of true culture. When he distinguished the man of culture from "the academic," he had someone very different in mind: the rare man of true culture and education, the *gebildeter Mensch* who has received and achieved *Bildung* (see note 13 to Lecture III).

7   Mostly forgotten in our day, the German Jewish writer Berthold Auerbach (1812–1882) was a famous man in his own time. Ivan Turgenev likened him to Dickens. Auerbach owed this reputation primarily to his five volumes of *Black Forest Village Stories*, the first of which appeared in 1843. These stories lovingly depict peasant life in Auerbach's hometown of Nordstetten, and they were much beloved—by all kinds of readers. Richard Wagner was a fan. Jacob Grimm credited the *Village Stories* with "curing him of his prejudice," saying that he "wouldn't have thought a Jew capable of penetrating the German soul so deeply." Coming across as German was a point of pride for Auerbach, who had once dreamed of being a rabbi, and during the Franco-Prussian War, he issued a patriotic pamphlet, which he went on tour to present. Nietzsche would later ridicule Auerbach's political writing in rather loaded terms: "I remember reading an appeal by Auerbach 'To the German People,' where every turn of phrase was convoluted and mendacious in the most un-German way. The whole thing amounted to a soulless mosaic of words written with international syntax." If Nietzsche read the *Village Stories*, they didn't cure him of anti-Jewish sentiment as effectively as they did Grimm.

8   Karl F. Gutzkow (1811–1878) rose to prominence as a member of the Young Germany movement, whose opposition to the repressive ways of the Prussian regime moved the parliament to ban the works of its authors (see note 12 to Lecture V). This happened in 1835, the same year that his best-known book appeared: the novel *Wally the Skeptic*, whose edgy content landed Gutzkow in prison for blasphemy. Heinrich Heine, a fellow Young Germany writer, thought highly of Gutzkow, referring to him once as "the greatest talent to emerge since the July Revolution" of 1830. But by the time of Nietzsche's lectures, Gutzkow had settled into a more sedate mode—realism with a social conscience—and had distinguished himself largely for his prodigious output. During the 1850s, he wrote two novels whose length exceeded four thousand pages, along with quite a few other books and journalistic pieces. Yet he was widely regarded as a serious writer, and his work thus epitomized what

Nietzsche took to be a major problem: a mass-produced culture of pseudo-elegance and superficiality enshrined as high culture. Elsewhere Nietzsche ridiculed Gutzkow as a "style monstrosity."

9 Georg Gottfried Gervinus (1805–1871) was a historian who wrote the first history of German literature, published in five volumes between 1835 and 1842 and focusing on the development of a uniquely *German* literature. Heinrich Julian Schmidt (1818–1886) was a gymnasium teacher, journalist, and prolific literary historian whose works include *The History of Nineteenth-Century German Literature*, published in 1855. By dismissing figures from opposite ends of the literary history spectrum—Gervinus the academic and Schmidt the journalist—Nietzsche is suggesting that there is little of value in the whole pursuit.

10 The idea of Greece as the "land of deepest longings" was, as Nietzsche suggests, a common theme in German classicism, found in Goethe's *Iphigenia in Tauris* among other places.

11 Friedrich Spielhagen (1829–1911), a defender of liberal pre–1848 Revolution ideals, was the author of several German realist novels, the most famous being *Problematic Characters* (1861), which was a literary sensation.

12 *The Journalists* (1852) is a comedy by the popular German novelist—and journalist—Gustav Freytag (1816–1895), whose works often served the function of instructing Germany's rising middle classes in the art of bourgeois living.

13 Hermann Grimm (1828–1901), the son of Wilhelm Grimm, was "called," as the Germans say, to a chair in art history, the first of its kind, at Berlin University in 1873.

14 The term Nietzsche uses here is *Humanitätsbildung*—that is, a type of education that forms young people according to classical ideals through the study of Greek and Roman culture. But here and elsewhere, especially in "Homer and Classical Philology" (1869), his inaugural lecture in Basel, Nietzsche pushed back against a German history of classicism extending from Johann Joachim Winckelmann's *Thoughts on the Imitation of Greek Works in Painting and the Art of Sculpture* (1755–1756) to the neoclassicism of Schiller, Goethe, and Humboldt at the turn of the century. Most of these earlier accounts emphasized the unity and grace of ancient Greek culture, claiming that the Greeks stood apart from the

moderns in their effortless embodiment of unity and simplicity. Nietzsche challenged this image of "noble simplicity" in *The Birth of Tragedy*, and, as James Porter has pointed out, more profoundly historicized classicism. Where German neoclassicists celebrated the unique and integrated Greek soul or mind, Nietzsche saw projections of modern ideals and desires, especially the longing for unity and wholeness. For Nietzsche, antiquity could never be reconstructed or resurrected in a unified image. It could only be accessed through fragments and glimpses, whose framing told us as much about the modern philologist as it did about ancient cultures.

15   Wolf (1759–1824) was one of the leading philologists of the late eighteenth century. He also played an important role in education reform—he eventually had a professorship but first worked as a gymnasium teacher and principal. Wolf, indeed, has been credited with making the gymnasium a "genuine educational institution" (an institution of *Bildung*). In preparation for his lectures, Nietzsche read, among many other things, a book about Wolf's pedagogical activities—J. F. J. Arnoldt's *Friedrich Wolf and His Relation to the School System and Pedagogy* (1862)—and came away admiring Wolf for having established a rigorous curriculum that aimed to instill in students a healthy reverence for classical culture.

16   Giacomo Meyerbeer (1791–1864) was a German Jewish composer known for his opera music, but perhaps is most famous as the object of Wagner's anti-Semitic smears in "Jewishness in Music," published in 1850. Meyerbeer had supported Wagner early in his career, as Wagner sought funds to stage *The Flying Dutchman* (a story Wagner had learned about from Heine, another target of "Jewishness in Music"). But Wagner turned on Meyerbeer and claimed that Meyerbeer's success was a function of his uniquely Jewish capacity to mimic high art in such a way that it appeals to the masses.

17   The Protestant Reformation stood out for Nietzsche as another point in German history when, as he put it, the German people drew upon something deeper, something beneath the events of the day, to transform themselves. He was not alone in this estimation: His reverence for the Reformation puts him in a long line of German thinkers and writers who grew up with Lutheran pastors as fathers, like Nietzsche's own, or who began their university life studying Protestant theology, as he did.

18 No doubt a reference to the recent Franco-Prussian War (1870–1871), in
    which Nietzsche, urged on by Wagner and his wife, Cosima, volun-
    teered to serve and worked briefly as a nurse.

LECTURE III

1   "Derived from the very nature of" something. Nietzsche is saying that
    they will be excluded on the basis of their natural character or disposi-
    tion.

2   "Like delights in like"—the opposite of "opposites attract."

3   A profusion of natural talent or genius. Nietzsche is making a pun of
    sorts between the Latin *ubertas* and the German *Ubertät*, profusion or
    fecundity, here translated as "excess."

4   There are echoes of Schopenhauer in this passage: "The production of
    genius—that is the goal of all culture."

5   For Nietzsche, *Volksbildung*, or "popular education," is actually an im-
    perative of the state, not of true education: it is in the state's interest to
    produce efficient citizens and an educated workforce. *Volksbildung*
    had been a common term since at least the latter part of the eighteenth
    century, when it referred to the spread of Enlightenment ideals such as
    freedom, toleration, and the dissemination of knowledge beyond the
    learned elite. Over the course of the nineteenth century, it came primar-
    ily to denote adult education and to refer to various associations that
    sought to educate those traditionally shut out from *Bildung* and *Wissen-
    schaft*, namely, the lower classes. Nietzsche included *Volksbildung,* along
    with freedom, equality, and compassion, in the list of modern ideas that
    were "wrong." For him, the goal of education was quite the opposite: to
    "help the noblest of one's contemporaries to develop."

6   Without the employment opportunities—or more precisely, the teach-
    ing opportunities—the classical gymnasium provided for their gradu-
    ates, university philological seminars would not have had as high
    enrollment as they did. With the early nineteenth-century changes in
    teacher requirements at the secondary level, the university arts and phi-
    losophy faculties, once way stations for the more professionally oriented
    disciplines of law, medicine, and theology, achieved both a certain self-
    sufficiency and a wider influence. At least through the first half of the

nineteenth century, university-trained teachers carried the ethos of academic specialization in the humanities beyond the university and into the gymnasium. And they helped institutionalize the assumption that the "advances" of systematic scholarship should guide pedagogical questions of method.

7   This line echoes a remark by Johann Voss, a friend of Wolf and an acclaimed translator of Homer: "We're turning out men who know everything about laying the foundations but forget to build the temple."

8   Hesychius of Alexandria (fifth century AD) compiled the largest lexicon of obscure Greek words to date. His *Alphabetical Collection of All Words* had more than fifty thousand entries.

9   Nietzsche is referring to the German tradition of critical philology that, among other things, had long since undercut the idea that the *Odyssey* was the work of a singular author named Homer. More broadly, he is challenging the assumption, held at least by the more neo-humanist philologists, that modern philology's demand for technical mastery was compatible with ethical cultivation. "By mastering and criticizing the variant readings and technical rules offered by the grammatical books and scholia," Wolf wrote in his *Prolegomena to Homer*, "we are summoned into old times, times more ancient than those of many ancient writers, and, as it were, into the company of those learned critics." The careful study of ancient manuscripts, scholia, and commentaries, according to preestablished methodological conventions, enabled a better understanding of the ancient world, which, in turn, facilitated an encounter with the moral exemplars of antiquity. But it also undercut the authority of the ancient text. Homer didn't write the *Odyssey*, argued Wolf, any more than Moses wrote the Old Testament. Wolf and the generations of German philologists who were formed in his image replaced classical models of moral authority with the authority of the modern philologist. For Nietzsche, this was one of the most disturbing things about the modern human sciences, especially philology.

10   The references here are to Sophocles's drama *Oedipus Tyrannus*.

11   Greek for "up" and "down." Nietzsche is mocking his fellow German philologists and only slightly exaggerating. Karl Lachmann, for example, one of the towering figures of nineteenth-century German philology, was celebrated for his discovery that the total number of verses of

the chorus and actors in every Greek tragedy was divisible by seven. Gottfried Hermann (see note 6 to Lecture II) wrote an entire treatise on the Greek particle ἄν, while Nietzsche wondered "what the teaching of Greek particles had to do with the meaning of life."

12   Aristotle makes this claim in his *Poetics*.

13   Nietzsche may well have had in mind the emergence of "big philology"—projects in classical scholarship that took shape in the 1850s and 1860s, which were sponsored by the Prussian Academy of the Sciences, and operated "on an industrial scale," as one of their leaders put it.

14   Nietzsche is likely alluding to a field-defining methodological debate between August Böckh's *Sachphilologie* (philology of objects/material culture), which consciously sought to include methods and knowledge from other fields, and the Leipzig philologist Gottfried Hermann's *Wortphilologie* (linguistic philology), which focused on grammatical knowledge derived from textual methods. The public battle over method began with Hermann's harsh review of the first volume of Böckh's *Corpus Inscriptionum Graecarum* (1825), which exemplified Böckh's conception of research as a large-scale project that "no individual could accomplish alone." Hermann facetiously asked why Böckh had been entrusted with the project in the first place, since it required expertise in ancient languages. The language of a people is that which "already in itself" characterizes the "essence" of a people, he claimed; the particularity of a people is best ascertained not through "insights into its mental and political life" but rather through a knowledge of its texts, the acquiring of which entails above all else "linguistic knowledge." In a direct allusion to Böckh and his students, Hermann wrote that the failure of contemporary philology lay in its general "disdain for linguistic erudition." So-called philologists like Böckh had never read the ancient writers in full and work merely from quoted and cited fragments, but from where, if not from the texts, could Böckh's purported insights come from?

15   The German for "pedantic" here is *mikrologisch*, a go-to term for nineteenth-century philologists who criticized their own field as hyperspecialized. But most philologists recognized the bind that philology had gotten itself into. On the one hand, specialized or "micrological" forms of labor, wrote Böckh, had made philology more productive and more distinct as a science. Philology should not be denied its "mi-

crology," just as natural science could not be denied its "microscopy," a specialization that had likewise led to new knowledge. But on the other hand, these practices and the kinds of research that they engendered threatened the philologists' sense of purpose. They were left wondering whether all this microscopic labor and specialization had blocked their way to large and meaningful questions.

16 The term Nietzsche puts in quotations marks, *Kulturstaat*, had gained currency over the course of the nineteenth century and referred to the close relationship between the state-building efforts of the Prussian government and the state-backed initiatives in education, science, and the arts. The term evoked, in particular, the state's attempts to treat culture as a domain from which the state could derive prestige and through which the state could extend its power. Prussia's first minister of culture, Karl Freiherr von Altenstein (1770–1840), considered the "culture state" the analogue of the "social state" and the "police state."

LECTURE IV

1 The *Realschule* (from Latin *res,* "thing")—a school to teach "real," i.e., objective and concrete subjects—was established as a parallel alternative track to the gymnasium, providing the traditional training in Latin as well as more practical training in the natural sciences and in economics. One of the first was the *Realschule* of economics and mathematics founded in Berlin in 1747. The "higher" *Bürgerschule*—"citizen school" —emerged in nineteenth-century Prussia, basically as a type of *Realschule*. In 1859, the Prussian government issued the first formal regulations for *Real- und höheren Bürgerschulen* (*Realschulen* and higher citizen schools) and established three different types of schools: a nine-year track ending in the exam required for university admission, a seven-year track with Latin optional, and a six-year, primarily vocational "citizen school."

Around the mid-nineteenth century, as frustration with the gymnasium's classical curriculum mounted, there was a conspicuous push for the creation of more *Realschulen*. These calls for reform pressured gymnasiums to become more "modern," in the sense of making them relevant for a technologically advanced society. There were even proposals to create a hybrid *Realgymnasium*, an institution that came into being in the 1880s.

In many ways, Nietzsche is simply recapitulating the caricatures of both sides of the debate. Defenders of the classical gymnasium dismissed defenders of the *Realschule* and *Bürgerschule* as vulgar materialists or industrialists, while the latter dismissed the former as entitled pedants.

2 Nietzsche is likely playing off the title of a magazine, edited by Karl Gutzkow, that published a lot of realist fiction: *Entertainment by the Hearths of Home*.

3 The "loyal Eckhart" is a figure from German heroic legends. In *Song of the Nibelungen*, he is a prophetic voice to his master, Hagen von Tronje, whom he helpfully warns to be on the lookout for the Huns.

4 These lines are from Part One of Goethe's *Faust*.

5 In *The Birth of Tragedy*, Nietzsche rejects a theory hazarded by the Romantic author A. W. Schlegel, according to which the Greek chorus was originally made up of "ideal spectators" from the audience. For Nietzsche, this represented a uniquely "Germanic" affection for everything "ideal."

6 "Nature does not make leaps": the idea, invoked by Leibniz, Linnaeus, and Darwin, among others, that transitions in nature are gradual and smooth, not sudden jumps.

7 Gotthold Ephraim Lessing (1729–1781) is best known today as the author of the drama, or plea for tolerance toward Jews, *Nathan the Wise* (1779), whose sympathetic eponymous character was modeled on Lessing's Jewish philosopher friend Moses Mendelssohn (1729–1786). But Lessing was also a slashing critic and freethinking polemicist, who struggled to make it as an independent writer and intellectual; it is this latter side of Lessing that appealed to Nietzsche.

8 Johann Joachim Winckelmann (1717–1768) is generally considered to be the founder of the discipline of art history. Of humble origins, he relied on patrons and worked as a librarian, in both Germany and Rome. Later, Nietzsche alludes to the fact that in Rome, Winckelmann worked for high-ranking authorities of the Catholic Church, who, before giving him a job, stipulated that he had to convert to Catholicism.

9 The German here is *Klötzen und Götzen*, a rhyme containing a clever bit of wordplay: Nietzsche is referencing Lessing's conflict with two rivals, C. A. Klotz and J. M. Goeze.

10   Friedrich Schiller (1759–1805) died of tuberculosis when he was forty-five. For years, though, a variety of conditions had afflicted his health. The doctor who performed the autopsy was astonished that Schiller had managed to live as long he did. All his major organs were badly damaged; in some cases, they were "unrecognizable."

11   In his epilogue to Schiller's "The Song of the Bell," Goethe eulogizes Schiller's refusal to succumb to the temptation to despise the ephemeral nature of our human existence. Schiller fought this tendency in himself, Goethe writes, by "Raising, through many a work of glorious birth / Art and the artist's fame up t'ward the skies / He fills with blossoms of the noblest strife, / With life itself, the effigy of life."

LECTURE V

1   *Et hoc genus omne* (from Horace's *Satires*): "and all that sort of thing."

2   These were regional courts in the Holy Roman Empire, whose authority was granted directly by the emperor. They were ad hoc judicial bodies convened to decide specific cases.

3   German university students generally enjoyed much more freedom and latitude than did their counterparts in American colleges, which throughout and beyond the nineteenth century operated according to the model of *in loco parentis*. Most U.S. colleges had at least some compulsory courses, while at German universities, there were no courses required of all students: a student's chosen field determined the course requirements.

4   Strictly speaking, this isn't true. In some fields, advanced university students took research seminars, whose emergence in the nineteenth century played a key part in driving the culture of specialization that Nietzsche's lectures decry. But lecture courses did constitute the bulk of instruction.

5   The lecture had a long history in German universities. As its etymology from the Latin *legere*, "to read," suggests, it referred to a "reading or dictation from an authoritative text." Similarly, the German term for lecture, *Vorlesung*, comes from *vorlesen*, "to read in front of." Reading and lecturing were deeply related, each grounded in the authority of the particular canonical text that was read. Through the process of selection

(and exclusion) the professor transmitted and safeguarded cultural information and traditions.

The medieval and early-modern lecture was, in addition, an occasion for students to take extensive notes, a crucial resource in a book-poor culture. Around 1800, this form of the lecture practice came under sharp criticism by figures such as Schleiermacher, Fichte, and Humboldt, who attacked professors for merely reading directly from a printed text. These thinkers advocated for a more performative lecture, in which the professor carried out the very act of thinking. As printed texts became more easily available, lectures had to do more than present content; they had to be creative and productive. Pushed by this new program, the lecture survived and even flourished as a mixed practice of reading, extemporaneous speech, and note-taking.

6   One of Humboldt's most consequential moves as a reformer of higher education was to lay out modern notions of academic freedom: the need for scholars and scientists to be able to pursue knowledge freely, and the need for students to have intellectual freedom in order to develop properly. These notions figure prominently in his plans for a new university in Berlin, and their adoption is one of the reasons why the resulting University of Berlin, founded in 1810, is commonly regarded as the first modern research university.

7   Of course, foreigners did visit German universities, and many of them embraced the very traits that Nietzsche's lectures are presenting as odd. Countless Americans who studied at German universities in the nineteenth century—Henry Tappan, James Morgan Hart, Andrew Dickson White—celebrated the principles of *Lehrfreiheit* and *Lernfreiheit*: freedom in both teaching and studying. The German elective system enabled professors to teach what they wanted to, at least for the most part, and students to study what they wanted to, taught by professors actively engaged in the pursuit of new knowledge. For some Americans, the only question was how to make it work in the United States—by 1872, Cornell, one of America's largest universities at the time, had already instituted an elective system that was inspired by the German model. But other American observers were less enthused. They pointed out that German students tended to make limited use of their freedom, often focusing narrowly on doing what they needed to do to get to and through the exam stage: university education was simply a means of pro-

fessionalization, right from the start. And while professors chose what to teach, it could be hard in this context to attract students to the courses they most wanted to teach. As Nietzsche's lectures point out, students helped dictate the curriculum. Was that a good thing? Moreover, hiring top researchers had its hazards, too. Some of the most eminent German professors treated the lecture as a time for working out new ideas and appeared to be talking to themselves rather than to, or even at, the students. Many were famously incomprehensible, such as the great historian Leopold von Ranke. Nietzsche, however, was considered an effective and conscientious lecturer, although after *The Birth of Tragedy* damaged his standing in his field, he had a very hard time attracting students.

8   The German literally means "to be able to lead themselves around on their leading strings [*Gängelband*]," an image Kant made famous in the Enlightenment context: We attain maturity and freedom by casting off the leading strings of others.

9   Nietzsche means Hegelian historicism. The line quoted later in the paragraph is from the preface to the *Philosophy of Right* (1835), in which Hegel famously posits: "What is rational is actual; what is actual is rational."

10   In his 1874 notes for a never-completed work, which he entitled "We Philologists" and intended to make the fourth essay in *Untimely Meditations*, Nietzsche wrote: "A big public lie. The ancients are truly our true masters and teachers; but not for the young. However, our gymnasium teachers (the best ones) do not care about that. They keep educating students to be scholars, or rather, they educate them to be philologists and nothing else. If we were honest, we would at some point have to turn the gymnasiums into scholarly academies for experts in historical philology."

11   The feuilleton is, as its name suggests, of French provenance. More precisely, the French journalist Julien Louis Geoffroy is the father of the form. On January 18, 1800, Geoffroy, an editor at the Paris-based newspaper *Journal des Débates*, started using the space left over on the paper's advertising insert for his own cultural commentary: *feuilleton* literally means "small sheet." The name stuck, and it continued to stick even after newspapers moved the feuilleton into their main body. Today, most major German-language newspapers still have a feuilleton section where, as

was the case in Nietzsche's time, one finds reviews, essays on culture and politics, short fiction, travel reports, and other things.

Starting in the late nineteenth century, the feuilleton became a lightning rod for abuse, particularly from anti-Semites. It was often treated as a decedent, fraudulent, un-German form that had managed to take over German culture. "What the Jews do today," one critic maintained, is "strip all discipline from thinking, sodomize the word, deflower and feuilletonize the intellect, and turn it into a prostitute in the newspaper and the market hall." According to Heinrich von Treitschke (1834–1896), to cite another example, Heine subverted the core value of German culture by making the feuilleton, that "foamy French passion drink," "sovereign" in Germany: After Heine imported the feuilleton model, Germans no longer "prized content over form." There was also a high-modernist critique of the feuilleton as a genre that dealt in false subjectivity; the feuilleton sounded personal, very much so, yet in truth it was anything but that. It was, rather, mass produced and formulaic. For Robert Musil (1880–1942), there was thus "only one reason" to write a feuilleton: "a paycheck." In short, the feuilleton took serious heat from different sides, with the strands of invective sometimes coming together. Hence Theodor Lessing's remark, in a feuilleton of 1929, that "the word 'feuilletonist' is the nastiest insult in the German language."

12 Self-consciously not Romanticism, and more politically engaged than German Realism, Young Germany was the major German literary movement between those two isms, despite partially overlapping with both. Its members included Gutzkow, Heine, Heinrich Laube (1806–1884), and Ludolf Wienbarg (1802–1872), whose 1834 work, *Aesthetic Battles* (the title sounds much better in German), popularized the name Young Germany. Wienbarg's book begins with the line: "I dedicate these speeches to you, young Germany, not to the old one." The movement was very much a phenomenon of the *Vormärz* era, the years leading up to the revolution of March 1848, when progressives felt hope for meaningful constitutional reform alongside their frustration over the repressiveness of the German lands, especially Prussia, in the age of Metternich. The Young Germany writers had the bitter vindication of illustrating the intolerance of the Prussian regime by becoming its victims. In 1835, Prussia enacted special legislation banning all their works, past and future.

13 A special kind of student fraternity (see note 11 to Lecture I), the original *Burschenschaft* was founded in Jena in 1815. Many of the early members were, as Nietzsche suggests, returning veterans. Inspired by the decisive victory over Napoleon in the Battle of Leipzig (1813) and the nationalistic ideas of Friedrich Ludwig Jahn (1778–1852) and Johann Gottlieb Fichte (1762–1814), but also disappointed by the resolutions of the Congress of Vienna, these student organizations promoted a conservative, Christian vision of a unified Germany whose core values would be honor, freedom, and fatherland, and where French influences would be discarded. Moral reform and religion (namely, Protestant Christianity) were seen as the key elements of nation-building. Indeed, the student movement notably came together on October 17, 1817, for a celebration of the three hundredth anniversary of the Protestant Reformation at the fortress in Thuringia where Luther had sought refuge in 1521. The movement was viewed as a threat and the government cracked down on the *Burschenschaften* in 1819.

Needless to say, Nietzsche is not unconditionally embracing the early *Burschenschaften*. He was far from sharing their Christian outlook. But for all his dwelling on the malaise of German culture, he was still basically a nationalist in 1872, and thought that Germany could revitalize itself by purging its foreign elements and bringing forth genuine national feeling, rather than the empty "self-flattery" of the French Second Empire. He wanted the true Germany to rise up.

14 In Schiller's first play, *The Robbers* (1781), Karl Moor leads a gang of young men back from the Seven Years' War to resist the tyrannical reign of his brother Franz. The second edition of the drama, published in 1782, included a frontispiece of a lion set to spring, over the motto *in tyrannos*, "against tyranny." Nietzsche might also be alluding to Schiller's play *Maria Stuart*, in which tyrants are said to tremble.

15 Tacitus wrote *Germania*, the original historical and ethnographic study of the Germanic tribes outside the Roman Empire, at the end of the first century. Kant introduced the quintessentially German idea of the categorical imperative in his 1785 *Groundwork for the Metaphysics of Morals*. In 1816, Carl Maria von Weber (1786–1826) set to music *Lyre and Sword*, a collection of patriotic poetry by Theodor Körner (1791–1813) who had fallen in the German War of Liberation; Weber's music was known

especially for the way it used instruments to recall the sounds of battle, with bugles and horns being prominently featured.

16   Karl Follen (1796–1840) was the leader of the *Burschenschaft* in Jena and advanced a "theory of individual terror" that provided a justification for political murder if one was genuinely led to it by one's conscience. The theology student Karl Sand (1795–1820) was influenced by Follen's theory, and he stabbed to death the writer and diplomat August von Kotzebue (1761–1819), believing that he was a Russian agent attempting to derail Prussian reforms.

NIETZSCHE'S INTRODUCTION

1   On the *Realschule* and gymnasium, see note 7 to Lecture I and note 1 to Lecture IV. *Volksschule* was a term introduced in the early nineteenth century for elementary schools open to all. Hence its name: "school for the people." During the first half of the nineteenth century, these schools proliferated in the German territories, where, by 1850, about 80 percent of children attended elementary school.

2   Nietzsche is referencing the appearance of the term *Urvaterhausrath*, itself something of a grandfatherly curiosity, in the first part of Goethe's *Faust*.

3   See note 11 to Lecture IV. Note that Schiller's *fighters* were artists.

NIETZSCHE'S PREFACE

1   "Contemplation of the possible forms of the future."

TITLES IN SERIES

For a complete list of titles, visit www.nyrb.com or write to:
Catalog Requests, NYRB, 435 Hudson Street, New York, NY 10014

* *Also available as an electronic book.*